Property

Concepts in Social Thought

Series Editor: Frank Parkin
Magdalen College, Oxford

Concepts in Social Thought

Property

Alan Ryan

University of Minnesota Press

Minneapolis

Copyright © 1987 Alan Ryan

Published by the University of Minnesota Press
2037 University Avenue Southeast, Minneapolis MN
55414.
Published simultaneously in Canada
by Fitzhenry & Whiteside Limited, Markham.

Printed in Great Britain

Library of Congress Cataloging-in-Publication Data

Ryan, Alan.
  Property.
  (Concepts in social thought)
  Bibliography: p.
  Includes index.
  1. Property. I. Title. II. Series.
HB701.R89 1987   330'.17   87–25538

ISBN 0–8166–1669–8

ISBN 0–8166–1670–1 (pbk.)

The University of Minnesota
is an equal-opportunity
educator and employer.

꙳

Contents

Acknowledgements

Most of my intellectual debts will be evident from my notes; I am, however, especially grateful to Quentin Skinner for some stimulating exchanges on Machiavelli and negative liberty, to the members of the Fabian Society's Socialist Philosophy Group for three years vigorous debate on markets and socialism, and to colleagues on the Liberty Fund project on the history of liberty for their comments on the essay which grew into Part One of what follows. I am more generally indebted to my colleagues at New College for intellectual stimulation and support, and, above all, to Kate Ryan and Sadie Ryan for their encouragement — and, on the bad days, for more forbearance than even a man checking his notes is entitled to demand.

Introduction

Some years ago, I published *Property and Political Theory*, which investigated arguments about the justification of the private ownership of goods, land and the produced means of production from Locke to Marx. This book is neither a summary of it nor an extended footnote to it, though it is more nearly the second than the first. It is an essay on topics I could not cover within the framework adopted there; some lead on naturally from the earlier discussion; some are prefatory to those I did discuss. There remain innumerable issues about ownership which I have not tackled there or here.

This volume appears in a series which aims to introduce readers to topics in social and political theory. It is not a comprehensive introduction like Andrew Reeve's *Property*, nor a comprehensive account of justificatory theories of ownership like James Grunebaum's, *Private Ownership*. The existence of these books has allowed me to concentrate on the connections between property and freedom in a variety of moral and political theories from Plato to Robert Nozick, contrasting classical and modern, political and economic, moral and sociological concerns as seems most illuminating. What follows is therefore introductory, not only in presupposing no prior knowledge of the subject, but in being no more than a sample of the issues which one might discuss under this rubric. My readers must judge whether this sample has whetted their appetites.

Many writers have noticed that there are at least two separable 'problems of property'.[1] The first is the moral problem of the justification of private ownership. Why should anyone own anything? Why should the particular people who own land, houses, stocks and shares go on doing so? What, if anything, would be wrong if the state expropriated all the current private owners of such things and took them into public ownership? Entangled in such questions are numerous conceptual questions about the nature of *ownership* and its difference from other rights. For instance, outside systems of slavery, employers may have contractual rights against their employees, but do not own them; yet English law for centuries treated a man's rights over his servants as a branch of property law, and regarded 'conjugal affection' as part of a man's property. A man did not own his wife, but he did own a monopoly of her services. It is at any rate interesting that the law found it natural to treat such relationships in proprietary terms, and it raises several questions about the equivalence or non-equivalence of ownership and other rights. Some of these are relevant to the moral issues at stake here. Robert Nozick's defence of an 'entitlement' theory of justice, and his attack on democracy, 'social justice' and the welfare state rest on an analysis which treats all rights as if they are property rights; we are free agents because we own ourselves. We are our own 'holdings' and we may therefore do what we like with ourselves just as we may do what we like with our bicycles or shares. It may be doubted whether this is a plausible account of rights in general. If property rights are very different from other kinds of rights, that has wide implications, both for defences of property rights in particular, and for the rest of the entitlement theory of justice.[2]

The moral issues which ownership presents are familiar enough — many of them revolve around the justice or injustice of the inequalities resulting from the private ownership of land, producer goods or means of subsistence. Some are 'structural' problems, built in to particular moral theories; for example there is a familiar tension between the utilitarian justification for recognizing private property at all — that without recognized property rights, prosperity is unattainable — and the considerations of individual desert which many people think ought to govern who-in-particular comes to own what. As was noticed some years ago, this parallels a tension in theories of punishment, where the utilitarian justification of deterrence and reformation is somewhat at odds with the desire that only the deserving should be punished. What if unjust punishment was still more effective in keeping the peace?[3] In one version of a utilitarian justification of private property — most eloquently defended by von Hayek — the great virtue of capitalist private ownership is that by making economic success and failure an unpredictable gamble it calls forth energies no other system can match, and secures greater prosperity for everyone than any other system. Yet if the economy is a lottery, the participants in it cannot be said to *deserve* the riches or the poverty they end up with, leaving us with the question of how to balance our desire for a high level of prosperity against our concern that justice should be done to individuals. John Rawls's much-discussed account of justice-as-minimax is a gallant attempt to resolve — or perhaps to dissolve — precisely this issue.[4] Hayek himself sometimes affects to think there can be no problem — that since the worst off are simply unlucky there is no injustice involved and nothing to discuss. At other times he concedes the difficulties of this position and argues as Rawls does that the existence of private property is justified by an appeal to the well being of the worst off person.[5] Robert Nozick's 'entitlement' theory of justice is best understood in the light of these anxieties as an attempt to dissolve the whole problem by insisting that whether or not the market economy prospers, and whether or not its outcomes coincide with our ideas about desert, justice is done if and only if people are entitled to their 'holdings'.[6] He avoids what I have called the structural tension between the utilitarian justification of property as an institution and our desire for justice in particular cases by subordinating everything to justice in particular cases.

Property and Political Theory tackled issues such as this as they appeared in the work of Locke and his successors down to Marx and Mill. Part Two of this volume is similarly concerned with moral justifications of the existence of property rights, mostly in the writings of more recent writers than those I discussed before. But I begin here with a second 'problem of property'. This second 'problem' is not that of justifying the very existence of private property, or fighting off attacks on the evils of different systems of property. This concern, too, might be said to be in the broadest sense 'moral' (in that good and bad political consequences provide morally powerful reasons for or against particular systems of ownership); more interestingly, it is a sociological and social-psychological concern. From Aristotle to Jefferson, and even nearer our own time, there has been a tradition of thought which associates political virtue in the citizen and stability in the state with the ownership of land and the cultivation of the soil. Sometimes, self-reliant small farmers have been seen as the backbone of the military power of the state; sometimes larger landowners have been seen as the repository of the senatorial virtues; sometimes it is the diffusion of stable 'real property' among the middle ranks of society which has been relied on.

Always the issue is the effect of different sorts of property and different degrees of wealth on the public-spirit, wisdom, and self-control of the several social classes. In eighteenth century Britain, the landed gentry was defended even by sceptics like Hume, on the grounds of its providing a bastion against royal absolutism and popular libertinism; Adam Smith, the prophet and theorist of commercial society, who is known 'to every schoolboy' as the enthusiast for competition and the marketplace was so much a creature of this tradition that he feared for the survival of the martial and civic virtues in a laissez-faire society, even while he defended modern, commercial society as the true home of liberty.[7] This is a 'sociological' concern inasmuch as the assumptions on which all such theories rely are sociological assumptions about the effect of different systems of ownership, different kinds of property and of the kinds of economy which these promoted on the characters and aspirations of, say, freeholders, large landowners, artisans or shopkeepers. By and large, though not universally, the terms of the debate linked individual virtue, the control of corruption, and the preservation of a certain sort of freedom. The classical republican version of this concern was already somewhat antique by 1776, when it was revived by the American revolution, but there are more modern claims about the freedom preserving virtues of systems of private property, and I discuss some of these below, with an eye to distinguishing them from their ancestors and (generally) preferring their ancestors to them.

As will be evident, the point of all this is anything but antiquarian. A whole tradition of thinking has apparently run out of steam and has left us looking for its replacement. In the twentieth century small farmers have supported extremist parties of left and right, the 'middle rank' of society has supported Fascism, Poujadism and various forms of American populism. There are many plausible explanations of the way the difference in context between classical Athens, eighteenth century France, and twentieth century Europe and America should make all the difference between our being able to rely on the small property owner for social ballast and our having every reason to fear that in conditions of social and economic instability he will rock the boat ever more violently. The point of reflecting on some ancient considerations is here to sharpen our sense of what is distinctive about our present concerns. It goes without saying that if other scholars had not engaged in a disinterested antiquarianism we would be unable to turn their work to our purposes.

I turn in the last section to a number of accounts of the evolution of property rights where we find that what seem to be issues in legal history soon turn out to have a heavily 'ideological' character. I distinguish — heuristically rather than exhaustively — between 'economic' theories which explain the transformation of ownership in terms of the 'needs' of rational management, 'enlightenment' theories which explain the transformation in terms of the gradual emancipation of individuals from the constraints of a simpler existence, and Marxist theories which explain property in terms of the alienated condition of pre-socialist man. Although history is best written with an eye to the past rather than the future, evolutionary theories have always served an ideological purpose, either to justify the present or to incite rebellion against it. I end, therefore, with a last glance at that perennial topic, Marx's vision of a propertyless world. It goes without saying that these three sections do not exhaust their subject matter. Nor do they divide it up in the only way possible. A writer like Marx bursts out of my framework as he bursts out of most others — one of the inspirations of his work was his passion for the classical conception of the citizen, a conception which he thought impossible to realize in a world divided by modern forms of private property, but one which was latent in the modern economy and might be realized (though very much transformed) with the abolition of private property, the state, the legal system, and our current illusions about economics, politics and ethics. Less protean thinkers also stretch the framework I here provide; there is a fruitful tradition of thinking of the liberal welfare state as concerned with 'citizenship' as well as 'mere welfare'; writers in this vein are modernists and indeed modernizers, rather than Rousseauists hankering after the golden age of the Roman Republic, which must mean that their conception of what a citizen is stretches any analogy with the concerns of Machiavelli and Rousseau. If I tread incautiously over much of this terrain, it is not always because I am unaware of its pitfalls. My aim is to engage my readers' interest in these arguments; there is hardly a paragraph which does not raise questions that would need a chapter of a comprehensive treatment.

PART ONE:

POLITICS PROPERTY,

FREEDOM AND VIRTUE

Plato and Aristotle: Communication Versus Moderation

The ancient Greek world was no stranger to class conflict. I do not mean by this only that the Greeks experienced economic class conflict in the sense of the day to day struggle of slave owners to extract work from their slaves, of landowners to extract more from their dependent labourers and so on — important though that obviously was.[1] I mean rather that the Greeks were all too familiar with civil war between rich and poor, when the numerous poor killed, exiled and expropriated the few rich, or when the few rich killed the leaders of the poor, took away their citizenship rights and altered the property laws to make life easier for the rich and harder for the poor.[2]

The modern reader, used to the idea that his or her goods can be distrained to pay his or her debts, but aware that imprisonment for debt was abolished in the last century as too barbarous to contemplate, is often shocked by the rigours of ancient law. Its harshness towards the debtor and the penniless poor was extreme; Greece and Rome both had the institution of debt-slavery, whereby a debtor who could not meet his debts had to surrender himself to his creditor to work as his slave; in Roman Law, his very body became the property of his creditor. After many years of strife, peace between rich and poor was not secured in Athens until the constitution drawn up by Solon provided that nobody could sell himself into slavery, and laid the burden of maintaining the destitute upon the whole city. 'First and most important of all, he forbade men to borrow money on the security of their own persons'.[3] Even then, Athens hardly experienced tranquillity. In these conditions, it was impossible not to ask how peace and political stability might be secured, and impossible not to notice that the inevitable conflict of interest between rich and poor was one of the greatest threats to that peace. Nor was it only a matter of preserving the peace within one city-state at a time. The sad experience of most Greek city-states taught them that threatened oligarchies often resorted to assistance from the rich of other cities in order to put down their own poor; though all cities aspired after independence and a life lived under their own laws, they were painfully aware that men would sacrifice legality and independence alike to their own private interests. Proud aristocrats and ebullient democrats were equally likely to cast covetous eyes on the wealth, lands and colonies of their neighbours.[4] The problem was more urgent in Athens than elsewhere. No doubt human nature as well as Athenian politics was much to blame for these sad facts, and the Athenians had a better title than most to claim that they were bringing freedom and enlightenment to the rest of Hellas; but some cities were notably more stable, less factional and less often embroiled in war than Athens. This suggested that they had hit on some principle of social organization that others had not.

Even the defeats and disasters of the Peloponnesian War did not persuade the Athenians of the virtues of a quiet life; oligarchical terror was succeeded by a democracy determined to keep the rich in their place. Socrates had risked his life refusing to help the Thirty Tyrants; he lost it when the democratic assembly convicted him of corrupting the young by unsettling their moral prejudices. His devoted pupil Plato never forgave Athens for the murder. For anyone who disliked tumultuous politics, Athens was intolerable — and poor, simple, self-sufficient Sparta correspondingly attractive. Plato responded to what he saw as the challenge to design a social order in which men would be public-spirited, not hell-bent on private gain, in which class-conflict could have no place and overseas adventures no attractions. Everything for Plato depended on the uncorrupted virtue of the ruling class. The recipe for securing their virtue which he offered by *The Republic* was characteristically uninhibited. Although

The Republic is best known for the doctrine that 'either philosophers must become kings or those who are now called kings must become philosophers'[5], Plato offers a great deal of down to earth advice about the way in which the pursuit of wealth and economic activity generally will affect the republic's chances of peace and longevity. Living in an Athens which had been at war, first with the Persians and then with Sparta and her allies, almost his first thought was how to escape further wars. The recipe he offered was later vastly attractive to Rousseau and many others — a wealthy state would be exposed to the greed of its neighbours, and would breed arrogance and ambition in its rulers; so self-sufficiency amidst austerity should be aimed at. External war would be averted, because there would be nothing to excite the cupidity of other states; domestic peace should be achieved by the same means — since rich men fall prey to the temptation to treat the poor as sheep to be shorn, those who were to rule the ideal state must sacrifice their personal possessions entirely. For good measure, they must also sacrifice family life and all that might tempt them to forget that in ruling the state they were also its servants.[6] 'First, none of them must possess any private property beyond the barest necessities. Next, no one is to have any dwelling or store house that is not open for all to enter at will. Their food, in the quantities required by men of temperance and courage who are in training for war, they will receive from the other citizens as the wages of their guardianship . . . . If ever they should come to possess land of their own and houses and money, they will give up their guardianship for the management of their farms and households and become tyrants at enmity with their fellow citizens instead of allies.'

The connection between the abolition of private property and the abolition of the family was not fortuitous. In all classes, the Greeks thought of property as family property rather than individual property in the modern sense. As Zimmern remarks, 'the Greeks set out from a different starting point. In their early world of tribes and brotherhoods and families no one thought of his own "rights" or questioned the claims of society. Practically everything that he had belonged to his kin. He would not claim his own life for himself if they asked it of him in time of need. Why should he dream of claiming his house or his field or his cattle?'[7]

This 'non-individual' view of ownership seems at first sight to suggest a world of communal property and individual unselfishness — just what Plato hoped to steer his republic back towards. In fact, the family-centred conception of ownership commonly produced something quite other than unselfishness. It could easily make individuals more rather than less rapacious; twentieth-century social scientists who have gloomily written of 'amoral familialism' — the peasant's obsession with the security of his own kin and his entire unconcern with any larger loyalties — and have thought it the curse of backward societies, remind us that most of us are more uninhibited in promoting our family's interests than our own. Plato knew too that family pride often offered a more tempting reason to sacrifice the public good for the private than mere greed did. Rulers might not merely exploit their subjects for economic gain; they would use the resources thus acquired to lead them into self-destructive adventures. Rich young men hankered after glory and led democratic Athens into disaster; their wealth made them proud — and greedy too. This did not apply to the man in the street, however. The common people were welcome to keep their personal possessions and the tools of their trade, and thus to have a little property at least. This could hardly be extensive, since Plato wanted little or no trade, deplored elaborate entertainments and thought peace of mind a greater good than any amount of the world's treasures. Still, the ideal republic would need feeding, clothing and arming; some economic activity was indispensable if the Guardians were to receive even their meagre 'wages'. The common people were to be so wholly under the tutelage of their Guardians that whatever corruption of the spirit their trades entailed would not be a problem. In any case, it was not on their virtue but on their submission that peace depended.[8] A low level of economic activity and the absence of all personal possessions — let alone farms, villas, ships or mines — among the rulers would simultaneously solve the two great problems of the conflict between private interest and public good and the conflict between rich and poor.

Plato did not suggest that poverty would of itself secure the Guardians' virtue — he was not a Rousseau who (sometimes at least) thought that uncorrupted natural man needed no more than the absence of temptation in order to be good. Nor was the virtue he aimed for a specifically *political* quality; he was not a Machiavelli who thought that the tough lives of the Swiss peasantry gave them a virtue which made them the only free men in the Europe of his day.[9] Austerity and military training matters to Plato because it gives the Guardians self-control, not because it turns them into patriotic republicans. Having no private possessions merely insulates the Guardians against selfishness. They attain their special virtue only after rigorous educational training, and years spent in military service. What this virtue is not easy to say. It was analytically connected with Plato's conception of justice; and that in turn is a matter of every person doing the job for which he or she is best suited. Political theories which concern themselves with 'virtue' of one sort and another differ in the degree to which they rely on the virtue of *all* the citizens or of some leading person or group alone — Machiavelli presents us with two theories of *virtù*; in *The Prince* the prince's *virtù* is all-important and in the *Discourses on Livy* the *virtù* of the whole people is said to explain the greatness of Rome. In the *Republic* it is a moot point whether everyone can attain to virtue, but at any rate it does not seem that owning property is of itself enough to destroy one's virtue. Plato sometimes seems to suggest that everyone in the republic possesses *some* virtue, because everyone occupies his or her proper place in the scheme of things — for we might say that if one of Nature's cobblers sticks to his last, he behaves justly and attains virtue. At other times he seems to suggest that only the Guardians really possess virtue, because only they — the Philosopher-Kings — have attained the knowledge of the Good and the True to which philosophy aspires, and so understand what Reason requires of them. On any view, they must end with a quite special degree and kind of virtue, since they rule others as the others cannot rule themselves, and do so in the light of their philosophical training. The property-owning, trade-pursuing ordinary people are governed by reason, but it is only, so to speak, accidentally; it is not *their* reason. Deprived of their Guardians, they would be lost.[10]

From our point of view, the important thing about Plato's ideas is the opposition they sparked off, and the temptation they offered over the next 2,000 years. Plato treated property as nothing but a source of trouble; the only way to sterilize its ill-effects on politics was to make the powerful propertyless and the propertied powerless; getting mixed up in the processes of production, exchange and consumption could do nothing for one's character — at least nothing but harm.[11] Plato's claims were deliberately at odds with the actual aspirations of both the upper and lower classes of his own day — indeed, of any day. Though he was certainly a conservative and an aristocrat, there was nothing in these arguments to appeal to any existing ruling class — for there was no way they could keep their wealth and social position and yet be fit to rule; and there was nothing in them to appeal to any subordinate class, either, since Plato insisted that what the plain man needed was to submit himself to the absolute authority of his superiors. In short, Plato offered a utopian response to the political problem he was faced with. Even when offering what begins as down to earth advice, his imagination was fired by the prospect of the wholesale transformation of the conditions of political life, not by the prospect of a more successful statecraft.[12]

The *Laws* back away from this drastic, 'clean-sweep' solution; there he agrees that communism is in fact impracticable. The *Laws* anticipate Aristotle's *Politics*, not only in this concession to common sense, but in arguing that since perfection is not to be found among men, and all political power inevitably corrupts, we should give up the search for an incorruptible ruling elite to whom we may entrust absolute power. We must look for a government of laws not of men. Even the method of analysis is largely changed. 'Plato's procedure is to take what exists and to work out its flaws. This is strikingly different from his procedure in the *Republic*, where the ideal state is more or less deduced from the requirements of virtue. The philosopher-rulers do their work with an eye to the heavens, rather than to surrounding states.'[13] All the same, the *Laws* makes only limited concessions to the emancipation of property from public control and no concessions whatever to commerce and money-making. The community of Magnesia is a community of farmers; it is self-sufficient and engages in no trade with other states. There is a quota of land determined by lot, and nobody may have more than four of these units, while the state ensures that any male citizen has one. Any property beyond the upper bound is simply confiscated. Innumerable agrarian radicals have hankered after something along these lines ever since. Farming is acceptable and trading is not for reasons which Aristotle repeats in his *Politics*, chiefly that trading involves handling money, and money-making encourages a limitless acquisitive urge which is intrinsically bad for the soul and disabling for the citizen's performance of his duties. The *Laws* has always been a neglected work, and justly so, for although it is true that Plato here admits that the utopian communism of the *Republic* is impracticable, he hankers after it, still; he continues to maintain that it is the best solution in principle, and deplores the human weaknesses which make it unusable.[14] Unlike Aristotle, he sees nothing to celebrate in the need to strike a *balance* between the private and the public, family and *polis*, and therefore has nothing to say about the most interesting issues in the politics of any moderately free society.

Plato's taste for the clean sweep was part of a conception of politics which is characteristically a philosopher's conception. It is the perennial attractions of that conception which make Plato — and to a lesser extent Aristotle — our contemporary still, rather than a figure of merely antiquarian interest. Plato thought of politics as a matter of applying self-evident, rational principles to particular cases; to put the same point in a less neutral fashion — abolishing property entirely was part of Plato's campaign to take the politics out of political life.[15] Plato's obsession with unity, and therefore with community of property was, as Aristotle said, not a desire for the perfect *polis*, but for no *polis* at all. Hence, even when Plato considers his second-best state in the *Laws*, he still visualizes a constitution imposed by *fiat*. In the *Republic*, everything is done by *fiat*. If property causes dissension, let there be no property. Whether the solution would work, let alone whether we might be able to persuade people to accept it by anything other than dictatorial means, is not a question that receives serious attention. Plato was by no means the last philosopher to succumb to this temptation. The political writings of Bertrand Russell are full of just the same assumption that philosophers with unlimited power would put into practice moral principles which no rational person could reject, different though those principles are from anything Plato would have cared for. Even when proposing a moderate, democratic guild socialism, the 'philosopher-king' style is to say 'let there be cooperative production with appropriate forms of ownership to sustain it.'[16] Lenin's conception of the relationship between the vanguard party of austere revolutionaries and the ignorant masses to whom they bring enlightenment is equally reminiscent of Plato's picture of the relationship between Guardians and common people, and his demand that the revolutionary shall abandon all private interests in the service of the revolution more than reminiscent of Plato's demands on the Guardians. The temptation to turn our back on the actual complexities of the societies we inhabit and canvass 'unworldly' solutions to political problems was no doubt felt before Plato. It has certainly been felt ever since.[17]

One of Plato's greatest achievements was to provoke Aristotle's *Politics*. In Aristotle we find arguments about the connection between wealth and political stability which, as Seymour Martin Lipset gracefully acknowledged in 1961, have stood up remarkably well over a period of 2,300 years.[18] Aristotle entirely repudiated Plato's conception of politics; certainly, the point of political life is the search for the common good; certainly, we wish to live well, that is virtuously, rather than in piggish contentment. But, politics is necessarily about conflict, though conflict with the aim of resolving conflict; there is a proper place for people sticking up for their interests, and a proper place for people sticking up for opposed conceptions of what justice and the common good require of them. Unlike any other creature, man is a rational and a talkative animal; that is why man alone is a political animal. Some other creatures are 'gregarious'; they naturally and thoughtlessly gravitate together in herds and swarms. Men do not; they live together on terms; and they discuss those terms over and over again.[19]

To suppose that philosophers could somehow short-circuit this process of discussion and mutual accommodation is absurd. It could not be done without eliminating the variety and diversity which make politics necessary in the first place. If philosophers *were* to find themselves in power, they would be no more able than the plain man to agree on the application of their principles to circumstances. Yet it is that adjustment of principle to circumstance which makes politics what it is, rather than a branch of geometry or some other abstract science. Politics is a matter of *practical wisdom*, rather than abstract philosophy, a matter of what has become naturalized in English as *nous*; it is, therefore, a business in which age and experience count for more than cleverness.

An understanding of politics must start from the reality men know. That includes their everyday economic activities and the sort of property on which these depend. Aristotle starts from a different context from that of any modern writer, however. The context of Aristotle's discussion of these activities and these forms of property is his view that a state is an association of *households*. This means that it is not quite true that Aristotle's discussion of property is a discussion of the economic bases of political life; Aristotle insists that the *point* of property is the maintenance of the family, and this gives the discussion a moral flavour which more directly economic accounts in later centuries would lack. 'It is clear that. . . the business of household management is concerned more with human beings than with inanimate property; that it is concerned more with the good condition of human beings than with a good condition of property (which is what we call wealth); and, finally, that it is concerned more with the goodness of the free members of the household than with that of slaves.'[20] In defending private (in this non-individualistic sense) property against Plato's attacks, Aristotle looks to its positive virtues. If things are to be used as nature intends, they need to be owned by someone who feels a personal stake in looking after them. Plato's belief that what belongs to everybody will be looked after by everybody is false; people will think it belongs to nobody and therefore nobody will care for it.[21]

The good sense of this view, which is as evident in the 20th century as in the 4th century BC, ought not to let us pass over too swiftly the alienness to us of Aristotle's views on what sort of property people may have, and what sort of people may have it. Aristotle takes it for granted that if citizens are to have sufficient leisure to take an active part in politics, slaves will have to do the drudgery for them.[22] Whether those who are slaves in fact are rightly enslaved worries Aristotle. If Nature was always successful in achieving her ends, slaves would be strong but stupid; since Greeks are capable of freedom, slaves would be non-Greek; and they would have been captured when they were on the losing side in a war they had started unjustly; their owners would be tall, elegant, clearly born to command, intelligent and ready to offer the slave a kind of friendship which would suit the slave's nature. 'The contrary of nature's intentions, however, often happens: there are some slaves who have the bodies of freemen — as there are others who have a freeman's soul.'[23] He says nothing about what we should do about this. Again, Aristotle takes it for granted that women have no part in politics at all, are dependent members of households, and are not economic agents in their own right. He insists (against Plato) that not all forms of 'ruling' are alike, and that husbands rule wives quite differently from the way owners rule slaves, but wives do not appear as potentially independent owners of property (which Greek society, like Roman, allowed them to be only under unusual conditions), let alone as potential political actors. Aristotle is interested in the effect of property and of economic activity generally on the political behaviour of a wholly male citizenry.[24] I do not defend Aristotle in this, save to observe that small scale societies whose dealings with one another were commonly interrupted by war would inevitably have seen a closer connection between citizenship and military capacity than the modern reader does.

Because economic activity starts with the family's efforts to secure its own subsistence, Aristotelian 'economic theory' almost wholly concentrates on that.[25] The distinctive point he makes is the one he erects on the basis of the claim that family life and the private ownership of land and the other means of subsistence is both a fact of life and the condition of things being looked after properly. Aristotle puts into circulation a view about the superiority of landowning and farming to trade or money-making which had a great impact on Christian economic doctrines after the assimilation of his philosophy in thirteenth-century Europe. Nature supplies things for use; mankind possesses skills which Nature intends to be used in improving and making use of Nature's other gifts. This is why property is natural to mankind, and a good thing. Moreover, all this has a proper natural boundary; there are limits to what people can healthily eat and drink; there are limits to how much house room they need; Nature's limits are so set that

exceeding them is not only wicked but also self-destructive —
gluttony and drunkenness bring their own retribution, to take
one instance.[26]

Farming is essentially concerned with creating things for use
rather than exchange; it is a way of making a living which
constantly reminds us what the proper terminus of our desires
is. Farming is therefore likely to breed a general temperance in
those who practise it; the virtues Aristotle wishes to instil in his
citizens are bound up with the need to make and obey law, so
justice and moderation are central. The benefits of farming
imply that it is not back-breaking drudgery — Aristotle is
thinking of gentlemen farmers rather than horny handed sons
of the soil, for in thinking of citizens, he is thinking of those
with enough leisure to go and take an active part in political
affairs. Still, it is important that farming is aimed at the use of
natural things in a 'natural' way. It differs crucially from
activities whose goal is the making of money; Aristotle thinks
that money is useful enough as a way of making barter-like
arrangements easier; but money is essentially 'unnatural' — it
cannot serve life directly, but only at one remove via trade.
Even extensive trade is illicit, 'because the gain in which it
results is not naturally made from plants and animals, but is
made at the expense of other men'. Aristotle's notion of profit
is essentially exploitative. The one economic activity which is
strictly unnatural in Aristotle's view is lending money at interest. 'The trade of the petty usurer is hated most, and with most
reason: it makes a profit from currency itself, instead of making it from the process of exchange which currency is meant to
serve.' It amounts to setting barren metal to breed, and to
breed more money at that; it is reprehensibly unnatural.[27]

Aristotle does not produce elaborate arguments to suggest
that money-lenders and merchants will be politically dangerous
— later ages did that over and over again — though it would
in general be in the spirit of his *Politics* to suggest that the
man whose livelihood is in something other than land is not
tied to his own city in the way the landowner is. Aristotle may
have taken it for granted that gentlemen would not wish to go
into trade or money-lending; over 2,000 years later Marx
explained the absence of developed capitalism in Athens in
terms of the lure of politics — rich men went into public life
and were not interested in making profits, so a technically

advanced society with high levels of literacy and developed skills in accounting and bookkeeping failed to make the economic leap which a scarcely more advanced England made in the sixteenth century.[28] Moreover, in Athens as in many other Greek cities much of the trade was in the hands of resident aliens, who had no prospect of attaining citizenship; Aristotle — though himself a foreigner — goes along with Athenian assumptions about the need to confine citizenship to the native-born.

Aristotle's contribution to the argument about the impact of property on politics is at its most impressive when he considers the causes of breakdown of political life or 'stasis'. He saw that the two 'scenarios' for civil war which plagued all Greek city-states were interestingly assymetrical; where an oligarchy felt threatened by the poor, they tried to convert their wealth into a political monopoly; where the poor felt threatened, they tried to convert their political rights into access to the wealth of the rich. Aristotle is no determinist; it is not the difference in wealth alone which is the direct cause of civil war, but the ideas about justice which that difference provokes.[29] The poor concluded that being equal in political power they ought to be equal in wealth; the rich concluded that since they were unequal in wealth they ought to have all the political power too.

Aristotle's remedy, which has been much admired by sociologists who have come across it since, was a distribution of wealth which would defuse the temptation felt by rich or poor. This distribution was what in the twentieth century has been called the 'lozenge' distribution. The intuitive thought is simple enough. If there are a few very rich people faced by a mass of badly off people, the contrast between rich and poor is very visible and irritating to the poor; and the rich are too few to stand much chance of defending themselves against any determined onslaught from below. If, on the other hand, most people have something like the median amount of wealth, things are very different; there is a steady gradation of wealth from top to bottom, people can aspire to move up a little, they will not be terrified of moving down a little, and egalitarian revolution loses its mass appeal, because too many people stand to lose as much to the people below them as they stand to gain from the people above them. Moreover, being a member of the 'middle rank' is good for the character. Of the middle classes, Aristotle wrote, 'They do not, like the poor, covet the goods of others; nor do others covet their possessions, as the poor covet those of the rich'; 'it is a further merit of the middle class that its members suffer least from ambition, which both in the military and the civil sphere is dangerous to states.'[30] They are secure, calm, unwilling to embark on adventures. It was a near cliché of the political sociology of the 1960s that the developed capitalist democracies had got to something near this condition, and that their political peace had much to do with the fact. Aristotle may be faulted for having less to say about how to achieve this agreeably tranquil state than about how agreeable it is if you do achieve it.[31] On the other hand, the sociology of political development is not so exact a science that we know very much more about it now.

There is one important distinction which we ought to draw between Aristotle's analysis and that of more sociologically — or merely sceptically — minded successors. His view of politics moves from social conditions to individual virtue and on to social peace, or from social conditions to class conceptions of justice to social strife; in asking, what sort of goodness must we inculcate in order to have peace, he offers as much a moralist's picture as a sociologist's. He does not suggest that we might preserve the peace by securing a balance of power between different classes or different groups who were themselves not particularly virtuous. If it is at all possible, Aristotle wishes the virtuous majority to swamp selfish or fractious interests; he does not trust a balance of not-very-virtuous forces to keep the peace instead. In this he differed from those other equally famous students of how to avoid *stasis*, the framers of the American constitution, who aimed to create political stability and freedom by ensuring that no selfish group could secure absolute power, not by trying to create a republic of moderate men.[32] The Federalists accepted many of his premises about the virtues of the men of stable wealth, and were frightened by the danger that the indebted poor farmers of their day would try to employ their political power to secure the repudiation of debt 'and other wicked projects' as Madison anxiously described them; none the less, they tried to ensure that even not very virtuous citizens would live in peace and prosperity. They had come to believe that 'faction' and 'party' were the price a modern society had to pay for its liberty, and set out to design a constitution in which each faction would check every other. Aristotle's account of what I have called the 'lozenge' theory of stability is not brutally sociological, appealing to nothing more than the fact that such a distribution is relatively immune to self-interested distur-bance. It rests on the idea that men of moderate means will be men of moderate ambition; men in such a position will not be tempted by arrogance or galled by poverty. They will be good citizens. Since Aristotle thought that the point of political life was the goodness of man in the *polis*, he concentrated his attention on what made for good citizens. The virtue of the good citizen was not straightforwardly a moral matter — as, of course, it very much was not in some of his successors in this tradition.[33] Nor was his interest in the citizen's character exactly the same concern with the 'individual' that we find in J.S. Mill or in twentieth-century writers in a similar vein. All the same, he was concerned with the citizens' souls, not only with the stability of a non-tyrannical republic. Whatever the ingenuity of Aristotle and the depth of his influence on later generations, we must distinguish his and their concerns pretty sharply.

One vital difference is the depth of his assumption that we live in a teleologically arranged world. The *polis* is prior to the individual, says Aristotle; man is born for life in the *polis*. Individuals and families are not self-sufficient; they have to be part of a *polis* which is self-sufficient, that is, which is of a size and kind to allow us to live well, and to live virtuously. The naturalness of the *polis* as an environment for a successful life explains why it is a premise of his view of political virtue that we are *born for* life in the polis, and this teleological perspec-tive equally explains his belief that the good life is a happy life. We should have no incentive to take part in the life of the *polis* unless it made us happy on the whole; but the argument is neither contractual nor individualist — the state is not a con-tractually established device to promote our individual inter-ests. We are happy *as the result* of living as we should.

This means that Aristotle's notion of the virtues of citizens is quite largely instrumental, and therefore both like and unlike what we tend to think of as 'moral' goodness; we must be moderate, public-spirited and scrupulous about justice —

manifestly 'moral' qualities — in order that the *polis* should continue and its members be able to live well. Being a good citizen is usually, but cannot always be, the same as being a good man. Aristotle anticipates Machiavelli in observing that it may be necessary for the sake of our own state to behave badly towards members of other states — we may need to lie to, fight with, or betray foreigners for its sake. More importantly, the virtue of the citizen is not the highest human good. Aristotle's conception of the very highest individual goodness stresses a degree of individual self-sufficiency at odds with his stress on the incompleteness of the citizen outside the *polis*.[34] Ultimate goodness is the possession of the philosophically enlightened man, whose goodness does not need earthly goods. It is the ordinary man who needs an adequate supply of worldly goods to live a decent life, and the best ordinary life is the life of the citizen; the *polis* exists for ordinary men who need land, tools, domestic animals and slaves — and political prudence teaches us what sort of property and what control of it makes for stability and virtue.

Finally, it must be noted that Aristotle has no great enthusiasm for the skills and energies of the politically active individual as we know him or her. Though Aristotle defends politics as he knew it against Plato's strictures, it remains true that in Aristotle's preferred *polis* not very much politics takes place, and his concerns are every bit as *defensive* as Plato's. The idea of politics as an exuberant search for glory, which makes Machiavelli such an invigorating thinker to read, is entirely foreign to him. The good polity shelters a good life, keeps out of excessive external and internal conflict, and allows us to lead lives of moderate comfort; it does not look on its subjects' property as a war chest, and does not aspire to cut a great figure on the stage of history.

Farmers and Soldiers from Machiavelli to Hume

Although Aristotle had observed that oligarchy and cavalry naturally went together — since it was an expensive business to breed horses — and that the naval forces and lightly armed infantry of Athens were a natural complement to Athenian democracy, he was not much interested in the art of war. The connection between property, military organization and constitutional theory became a central preoccupation of political theorists only after the Renaissance.[1] It was, of course, a pressing practical issue at all times. The Roman practice of giving farms to ex-soldiers and establishing military colonies throughout the Empire was one answer to the familiar problem of paying for an army. It eventually had destructive consequences, as soldiers followed their generals in the hope of gain, even when their generals were bent on subverting the existing political regime. The structure of feudal society, in which tenants held land in return for military services, was again in principle wholly determined by the arrangements made for the provision of armed forces. Yet, political argument in the middle ages did not revolve about the implications of that fact. The ideology of medieval kingship, borrowed from Christian sources, appealed to principles of mutual obligation based on oaths of allegiance on the one side and coronation oaths on the other, or appealed to the customs of the people and the reason enshrined in them. What was lacking was the dispassionate analysis of what it meant for a political society to meet its military needs by a particular system of property. To engage in that analysis required three things — a clear perception of the problem, the recovery of the classical concern with the maintenance of a republic, and political conditions which made self-preservation a pressing concern for separate states. It is outside the scope of this book and the competence of its author to decide when exactly those conditions were first met.[2] But there is no doubt that in the writings of Machiavelli the argument is spectacularly set in motion, and that after Machiavelli's account of the relationship between landed property, civic virtue and military effectiveness, his formulation of the issue largely determined later discussion.[3]

Machiavelli's discussion of *virtù* catches the eye because of the discrepancy between his conception of *virtù* and the ordinary notion of virtue. Among the elements of *virtù* which Machiavelli discusses in *The Prince* are such things as cruelty, a willingness to lie, kill, break oaths, and much else of the same sort. 'A prince, and especially a new prince, cannot observe all those things which are considered good in men, being often obliged, in order to maintain the state, to act against faith, against charity, against humanity, and against religion.' Neither the Christian conception of the virtues nor classical ideas of virtue — as described by Aristotle or Cicero or the Stoic moralists — could possibly embrace evil in this fashion. This, however, was not because Machiavelli wished to convince his readers that their ordinary moral views were simply mistaken. Rather, he was concerned to point out that *if* they tried to adhere to the demands of morality, they would, not always but much too often, fare badly. Rigid adherence to Christian virtue is politically disastrous. This means that Machiavellian *virtù* is to be understood in wholly instrumental terms. It is the set of abilities that makes for political success and the achievement of glory. Thus, cruelty was part of Hannibal's *virtù*, for instance, not because cruelty is a good thing in itself, but because cruelty is usually indispensable to preserving order in an army. 'Among the noteworthy actions of Hannibal is numbered this, that although he had an enormous army, composed of men of all nations and fighting in foreign countries, there never arose any dissension either among them or against the prince, either in good fortune or in bad. This could not be due to anything but his inhuman cruelty, which together with his infinite other virtues, made him always venerated and terrible in the sight of his soldiers.'[4]

Here we may ignore Machiavelli's treatment of the *virtù* of the prince, since that discussion is avowedly concerned with the establishment of new states, where everything depends on the skills of the prince himself. It is in his *Discourses on Livy* and *The Art of War* that Machiavelli lays down the principles of sound statecraft and military preparedness, and connects property, military effectiveness and political liberty in the fashion that so influenced his successors. It must be said, however, that they are all of a piece with the advice offered in *The Prince*, as he insisted. The basic principles he establishes are simple, and, he claims, backed up by the best Roman practice. A popular republic exists to preserve liberty; this liberty is of two sorts — immunity to interference by outside enemies and freedom from internal tyranny. The Roman republic is the greatest example of such a republic known to mankind, and reflection on Roman practice is the key to sound statecraft; an important part of that is to secure economic conditions which will support an effective militia.[5] In principle, Machiavelli allows that a successful republic might pursue a variety of political goals, though these largely reduce to the thought that a state might aim for longevity or for increase. He took the imagery of 'the body politic' seriously, and conceived of the constitution as whatever made for the political equivalents of health and strength. A long and vigorous life was the obvious standard of success. The Roman republic, however, impressed him so much that it is doubtful whether he really took mere preservation as seriously as the pursuit of glory through expansion. Roman freedom was preserved by the *virtù* of the whole people, displayed most prominently, but by no means exclusively, in the stunning military successes of the republic. The intriguing question is what it consisted in and how it was preserved by the system of property.

The polar contrast is between virtue and corruption. Corruption is the state of affairs which obtains when men prefer their private interests to the public good, when individuals become so rich that they can buy the services of their fellows and divert them from the service of the polity, and others become so poor that they have to become the clients of rich men. When men are corrupt they will not fight for their country; the rich will fear for their lives and will wish to hire mercenaries; the poor will have lost their stake in the country and will have nothing to fight for, so mercenaries will be needed to replace them. But mercenaries are disastrous. Since they fight for a living, not out of patriotism, they will flee for their lives if things get dangerous; and if they are successful, they will be tempted by the thought that they can take over supreme power and add its rewards to their existing pay.[6] The evidence of the Romans who prospered by not using them and the Italians of his own day who suffered constant disaster by using them seemed to Machiavelli quite incontrovertible. The Roman soldier fought for his own farm, to which he was attached by ties of self-interest and religious devotion alike. It is characteristic of Machiavelli that he admits that there is a sort of tragedy implicit even in this recipe. Toughness will breed military success; that will create prosperity and enable rich men to appear; that leads to corruption.

The recipe for republican virtue is, then, to work on the human raw material in such a way as to breed patriotic citizens and tough leaders whose ambitions will not lead them to corrupt their fellows and overthrow the free constitutional order. The main implications for the economy are that landed gentleman — 'grandi' or 'gentiluomini' — are the death of liberty, and a society of austere freeholding farmers its best support. The government of the state and the waging of war take up time, however, so it was no use founding a republic in a place where all the citizenry's efforts had to go on merely feeding themselves. The secret was to choose a location which would allow a reasonable living, but to restrain trade and other forms of economic activity so that the people would live as austerely as in a harder environment. 'As it has been observed that virtue has more sway where labour is the result of necessity rather than choice, it is a matter of consideration whether it might not be better to select for the establishment of a city a sterile region where the people compelled by necessity to be industrious and therefore less given to idleness, would be more united and less exposed by the poverty of the country to occasions for discord.' He decides that 'a city should placed rather in a region where the fertility of the soil affords the means of becoming great, and of acquiring strength to repel all who might attempt to attack it, or oppose the development of its power . . . . the laws should compel men to labour where the sterility of the soil does not do it.'[7] In the second place, the state had to reckon with the natural badness of human nature. Men are by nature evil, and will only behave well when they are under constant pressure to do so. Self-interest cannot be stamped out entirely, either; there is no point in trying to do something so self-defeating, so it behoves a republic to ensure that the state is much richer than any of its citizens, so that it can always give greater rewards to any subject than the disaffected ambitious can.[8] The third great help is that of religion, and Machiavelli praises the Romans for their worldly, unsuperstitious but properly reverential outlook. They stamped on overt mockery of religion, but were not above rigging oracles and auguries when necessary. Their religion was firmly attached to the household and the farm, reinforcing the ordinary man's belief in the sanctity of tradition and the sanctity of family life.[9] Independent freeholders, used to hard work, bred to put up with discomfort and an absence of luxury, were the backbone of an uncorrupt republic and an invincible army. Americans have been tempted by such an image of the virtuous republic since long before the revolution.

Conversely, the Romans went to all lengths to avoid the creation of 'gentiluomini', the idle and ambitious upper classes who were the greatest threat to the freedom of their fellows. The ordinary people were, said Machiavelli, unambitious, and 'an immense majority desire liberty so as to be able to live in greater security'. They were not spontaneously great defenders of liberty, because the unorganized ordinary people were cowardly and lacking in initiative.[10] In Rome they had been properly organized and led, and were therefore anything but cowardly and ineffectual. Even in a relatively unorganized state, so long as their morale was high, the common people could do something to preserve internal liberty. Unlike Rousseau, who feared disorder and praised the Romans because they took such care to make *constitutional* arrangements to allow the simple and uncorrupted common man to check the ambition and giddiness of his superiors, Machiavelli was prepared to accept a certain amount of uproar as the price of liberty. Thus he argued that class conflict was not inimical to freedom and instanced the conflict between the plebeians and the patricians which checked the disposition of the upper classes to oppress and exploit the poor. 'I maintain that those who blame the quarrels of the Senate and the people of Rome condemn that which was the very origin of liberty, and that they were probably more impressed by the cries and noise which these disturbances occasioned in the public places, than by the good effect which they produced.'[11] Until the republic began to decay, there was always an implicit last resort to popular uprising and not infrequent actual resort.

Commentators argue about the influence of this tradition of thought. Machiavelli himself was simultaneously reviled as a scion of the Devil and plundered as a judicious student of stable government. In England at any rate, his concerns reappeared in the writings of Francis Bacon and at great length in Sir James Harrington's *Oceana*.[12] They were readily naturalized to an English context; for the Roman farmer and the English yeoman played the same role in Machiavelli on the one hand and Bacon on the other. In his essay on the 'True Greatness of Nations' Bacon advises that 'States that aime at Greatnesse, take heed how their Nobility and Gentlemen, doe multiply too fast. For that maketh the Common Subject, grow to be a Peasant, and Base Swaine, driven out of Heart, and in effect but the Gentleman's Labourer.' The success of the English in their wars with France had proved a military and an economic point: 'the Middle People of England make good Souldiers, which the Peasants of France doe not.' The advice boils down to 'keepe the Plough in the hands of the Owners, and not meere Hirelings'.[13] Harrington's ideas are less easily summarized, because he employed not only the old opposition between virtue and corruption and the old enthusiasm for the armed farmer, but an idea which certainly appears in earlier writers but plays nothing like as large a part, that of the 'balance'. One could, stretching the evidence, credit Machiavelli with an insight into the idea that social stability required that the balance of political power should follow the balance of property — but it would be a stretch. If Machiavelli thinks in terms of balance, it is rather in terms of a balance of opposed forces — aristocratic ambition on the one side and plebeian insistence on not being reduced to servitude on the other. It is perhaps more sensible simply to observe that if Harrington's idea of a balance is the innovation in political understanding that matters most to him, it is the traditional defence of land versus mobile money, of a citizen militia versus a standing army, of country virtue versus citified corruption that his successors learned from him. The nineteenth century alliance of radicals and Tories dismayed by the Industrial Revolution has its intellectual roots in what became the ideological conflict of Court and Country.[14]

Harrington's notion of the balance is part of an attempt to rescue 'ancient prudence', by which he means the political analysis of Aristotle, Polybius and Machiavelli; equally, he is concerned to criticize 'modern prudence', by which he commonly means Hobbes. Ancient prudence perceived that there could be a 'government of laws, not of men', which Hobbes had denied by insisting that 'law is the word of him that by right hath command', and had understood, though inexactly, that its preservation was a matter of arranging agrarian property so that it sustained a 'commonwealth' or popular republic, rather than a despotism or an oligarchical tyranny.[15] Harrington's recipe for the purpose is reminiscent of the *Laws*, namely a division of land which will settle as much of the population as possible as independent freeholders, and confiscation for estates yielding more than £2,000 a year — unless they have been received as the result of inheritance (itself subject to elaborate restrictions which we may ignore). What underlies Harrington's emphasis on the agrarian law is the belief that ever since antiquity the crucial question facing governments is how to pay for the army; as we have seen, the Roman method eventually led to the downfall of the republic, and Harrington follows Machiavelli in demanding a citizen militia. Unlike Machiavelli, he does not carry his hatred of the 'grandi' to the lengths of denying the utility of cavalry, but argues that landowners worth £100 and upwards should provide cavalry, and the others the infantry. Like Machiavelli, however, he insists that the preservation of the state depends absolutely on the preservation of the virtue which he hopes to flow from Oceana's agrarian law.

Viewed as a solution to the questions he set himself — the achievement of stable republican government and the support of the armed forces of what he asumed was an expanding republic — Harrington's proposals are almost entirely unpersuasive. It was perhaps nothing more than bad luck that led him to assume that the monarchy would never be restored in Britain. He was writing in the 1650s when it was not implausible to believe that Britain would remain a republic. At the theoretical level, however, it was already apparent that Holland had preserved its liberty while relying on trade rather than land, and that Harrington's hostility to the 'easy come, easy go' of the marketplace was nostalgic rather than scientific.[16] Nor did it appear that the impossibility of financing their armed forces was about to bring the Dutch to their knees. The Dutch were capable of maintaining an army which could secure independence from Spain and a navy which could contest supremacy at sea with the British Navy; Charles I may have been brought down by trying to levy unpopular taxes to support his armed forces, but there was no sign that the Dutch government would suffer the same fate. It is, as I shall show in the third chapter of this part, easy enough to see what sort of arguments can be developed from 'Harringtonian' premises about independence and dependence once they are detached from the thought that attachments to the land are indispensable. Here, it is enough to observe, first that there is obviously something to be said for the obsession with land, namely that the soldier whose attachments are to some portion of the homeland, which he sees as his own, is likely to feel greater loyalty to his country than the soldier recruited only for pay, second that Harrington's own formulae owe much to a curious combination of nostalgia for Rome and an enthusiasm for an expanding Britain, which would colonize and settle Ireland and America — so raising the question of how to distribute new land.[17]

We cannot leave the issue there, for Harrington's use of the idea of a balance, and his tying it to classical ideas about corruption, allowed the eighteenth century to argue at great length about the dangers of the English constitution tipping over into absolute monarchy propped up by a standing army and sustained by a corrupted oligarchy enriched by dubious financial manipulation or, alternatively, slipping into a disorderly democracy. Hume was an astute commentator on this argument. He was acutely aware that no sociological generalizations about what political structure is compatible with what economic foundation are likely to be exactly true, and he began his essay on the question 'whether Britain inclines more to absolute monarchy or to a republic' by reminding his readers that Harrington had no sooner asserted 'that the balance of power depends on that of property' and that monarchy was therefore impossible in Britain, than Charles II was restored to the throne.[18]

However, Hume saw that there was much in Harrington's view if it was not taken too literally. In particular, a smaller amount of property concentrated in one man's hands would give him more power than a larger amount scattered among many hands; few sovereigns have possessed anything like the wealth of their united subjects, but most have been able to hang onto their power. Britain, Hume thought, was in balance, because the power of the king, resting on taxes, the civil list — which stern republicans denounced as a device for corrupting Parliament, which it certainly was — and his own fortune, just about allowed the monarchy to hold off popular pressure. Because Hume was more detached, more sceptical, and perhaps wiser than many of his contemporaries, he understood that a great variety of different traditions of thought converged on the same basic idea. The 'mixed constitution', blending monarchical, aristocratic and popular elements, had always been a favourite nostrum of English constitutionalists; one could argue endlessly whether what was crucial about the mixed constitution was its dependence, sociologically speaking, on the existence of a balance of property, or whether the attractions of the idea of balance were simply another version of the defence of a mixed constitution, that is, of the idea that a constitution which combined elements of monarchy, aristocracy and democracy could benefit from the strengths of each without incurring the weaknesses of any.[19]

Hume did not so much 'represent' as play with and speculate on the consequences of, two different pictures of politics. One was the civic tradition which Harrington had associated with 'ancient prudence', the other a much more modern understanding of politics as the interplay of legitimate economic interests within a settled legal framework. The first appeared in Hume's own scheme for a 'perfect commonwealth', which he freely admitted was not 'immortal' as Harrington's *Oceana* had aspired to be, but which none the less included a scheme of graduated representation, so mimicking the mixture of democratic, aristocratic and monarchical elements in the theory of mixed government, and based representation on property, so picking up Harrington's idea that the balance of constitutional right ought to match the balance of property.[20]

Hume went rather further than this in turning the analysis of this civic model to new purposes by admitting a positive role for what its critics would have denounced as 'corruption'. In so doing, he was following the lead of Bernard Mandeville, whose *Fable of the Bees* had provided a scandalous, but extremely effective demolition of the doctrine that private property was inimical to public good, that liberty and constitutionality depended on the virtuous self-discipline and self-control of the freeholding citizenry, and that new forms of property, such as stocks and bonds and government debt were the road to despotism and ruin. Where unbending enthusiasts for the rigid republican virtue of the older Cato thought all private interests inimical to the state, Mandeville had argued, first that the repression of self-interest was impossible, second that consistently achieved it would result in economic catastrophe, third that there was a new kind of liberty to be had in a 'corrupt' society.[21] He was, though the fact could hardly have been evident before Rousseau's *Discourse on the Origins of Inequality*, the great defender of the view that in shedding our 'natural' animal condition, we had become free agents.[22] Animals were mere consumers of what they needed, prompted by self-love — as men were too — to seize and eat what they needed, to flee their enemies and reproduce their kind. Human beings, because they were capable of envy, jealousy, sexual fantasy, pride and sheer silliness, were capable of acquisitiveness, of imagining and creating new objects, new ways of making things, new objects to covet. It was this which made them free of their environment in a way no animal other than man could be. Rousseau analysed the human condition in the same way, but with despair at the disordered state of the civilized psyche. Hume was, in this context, uninterested in scandalizing opinion in the way Mandeville had done, but equally quick to see what one might call the unintended public benefits provided by the pursuit of private interest. Nor was this only a matter of prediscovering what Adam Smith labelled 'the invisible hand' by which every man's self-interest was made to serve every other man's self-interest in the marketplace.

Hume's claim was that what others condemned as 'corruption' could preserve liberty and maintain the precarious balance of social forces. If one was, as Hume either was, or affected to be, fearful of the democratic pressures implicit in a parliamentary regime, the crown's control of office, and the king's ministers' control of office and access to economic opportunity was a form of 'property' which might balance the preponderance of property in land and goods held by the ordinary people. Moreover, Hume found a positive role for luxury which neatly took the wind out of the sails of the classical republicans. They denounced luxury while praising the 'middle rank'; Hume asserted that luxury enlarged that middle rank. 'Where luxury nourishes commerce and industry, the peasants, by a proper cultivation of the land, become rich and independent: while the tradesmen and merchants acquire a share of the property and draw authority and consideration to that middling rank of men, who are the best and firmest basis of public liberty. These submit not to slavery, like the peasants, from poverty and meanness of spirit; and, having no hopes of tyrannizing over others, like the barons, they are not tempted, for the sake of that gratification, to submit to the tyranny of the sovereign. They covet equal laws, which may secure their property, and preserve them from monarchical, as well as aristocratical tyranny.'[23]

Hume thus turned the argument against those who looked back to the ancient republics as the true home of liberty. He equally effectively turned the argument against Rousseauian assaults on modern corruption. Before leaving this subject, it remains to observe that Hume's argument was probably not original in his day, and has certainly turned up frequently thereafter. Many nineteenth and twentieth-century writers have taken a leaf out of Hume's book by pointing out that one of the advantages enjoyed by wealth is the way it commands deference; less often, but to considerable effect, he has been followed in his astute and worldly analysis of the benefits of corruption. To take only one familiar and perhaps overworked instance, Robert Merton explained the rise and success of the so-called 'boss system' in American politics in terms which Hume would have enjoyed.[24]

At the turn of the century, American cities were flooded with immigrants from Eastern Europe, Ireland, Italy and

Germany; they were often illiterate, bewildered by their new
surroundings, hopelessly at sea in cities like New York and
Philadelphia which were about as different as could be imag-
ined from their own rural backgrounds. They could easily
have formed a proletarian rabble ready to march to whatever
tune agitators sang. Instead, they were seized upon by political
agents who traded the votes of the immigrants for jobs, housing, help in hard times. It was, of course, utterly corrupt;
the politicians who gained office on their votes fleeced the
city treasury and lined their own pockets. None the less, they
integrated the newcomers into the American economic and
political order in the absence of any more structured and
uncorrupt way of doing the job.[25] Private interest produced
social benefit. The mode of analysis is essentially Humean or
Mandevillian. Middle class moralists denounced the boss
system but would not pay to buy it out, just as Mandeville
would have expected. Working class voters supported the boss
system as long as it provided jobs and welfare when the official
governmental system would not do so; as Hume would have
expected, moralizing did not kill it, but full employment and
social security did.

3
'Modern Liberty' and Property

It is a commonplace of 1970s and 1980s conservatism, or 'neo-liberalism' as it perhaps ought to be called, that private property is the basis of liberty. At its simplest, the argument is that although there have been many places in which tyranny and private property coexisted — South Africa, Tsarist Russia and Nazi Germany for three — the only places where liberal democracy flourishes are countries with capitalist economies. This is the argument offered by Milton Friedman.[1] It is also a commonplace among commentators and social theorists that the 'liberty' that such neo-liberals seek to protect is distinctively 'modern'. Between the eighteenth-century's 'classical' conception of political liberty and the modern conception of liberty and its dependence on property there is a great gulf. More exactly, the thought is that the ancient 'political' conception of liberty as citizenship, with its concomitant connection of military service, political participation, economic independence and individual 'virtue' has steadily given way to a 'negative' conception of liberty, which is 'political' only in the sense that the role of the state is understood as essentially a matter of protecting the rights of individuals. Among the most important of such rights is property. We can by the same token say that the political role of property has been transformed, too. The 'political' conception of property sees the ownership of land and arms as the condition of citizenship, and is hostile to money-making; the modern conception of property sees it as an *economic* resource, is friendly to money-making, and regards the demands of the state as a drain on resources and a threat to a man's right to do as he will with his own. Freedom is most vitally 'immunity to the service of the commonwealth', and as Hobbes and von Hayek have alike insisted, it is only contingently connected with forms of government. A *laissez-faire* dictator would grant us more liberty than an interfering democracy.[2] This modern conception of liberty connects *all* forms of private property with liberty, because liberty is primarily non-interference, and ownership is rightly understood in terms of rights over resources which the individual can exercise without interference. 'For I truly have no property in that which another can by right take from me, when he pleases, against my consent,' wrote Locke;[3] liberty is an individual possession, and a person's freedom is coextensive with what he may do without asking permission or fearing reprisals. A society dedicated to liberty achieves it by respecting individual property; we thus have two parallel arguments, linking constitutional government and property. Prosperous, private-property based economies preserve constitutional liberty, and the task of the constitution is to preserve our liberty to do what we will with our property.

Many liberal thinkers start from the belief that there are only two ways of organizing society's affairs, the first by way of the coercive dictates of a central authority, the other by way of the freely arrived at contracts of individuals who agree to transfer to one another their rights over whatever it might be: their time, their skills, and above all their goods. Liberty, justice and utility are maximized by reducing the role of the first to a minimum.[4] In the exegesis of the liberal tradition commentators draw a line from Locke through Herbert Spencer to modern defenders of a natural right to property such as Robert Nozick, the last of whom explicitly appeals to this lineage in situating his own work. Opponents of the tradition, such as Hannah Arendt and Sheldon Wolin, just as frequently accept the picture of it which is thus presented, but bemoan the loss of participatory liberty.[5]

It would be absurd to suggest that this widely held view of the liberal tradition and its differences from classical republicanism is simply false. It is less absurd to suggest that it is not entirely accurate. It is to that suggestion that the rest of this section is devoted. We must approach the question from three directions: first, was the old tradition, which connected property and liberty by way of an insistence on the need for citizen virtue, as deeply committed to political participation as implied by the writers who have condemned liberalism as they understand it — was it as unequivocally committed to 'positive' liberty as has often been said?; second, has the modern liberal tradition been so uncommitted to participatory liberty and political virtue as they suppose — has it been entirely founded on a negative conception of liberty and an obsession with private rights?; third, even if there is much in the contrast between ancient 'positive' liberty and modern 'negative' liberty, *can* the defence of 'modern' liberty rely on nothing more substantial than constitutional arrangements which restrict the state to a 'nightwatchman' role in the way of defining and policing property? If we answer no to these questions, we may have to recognize that modern liberty is a more complex ideal than is sometimes thought, and that modern liberals have been, and must be, better defenders of a positive, participatory and political, conception of liberty than they have always intended.

The classic account of the difference between ancient and modern liberty is Benjamin Constant's *Essai sur la liberté des anciens comparée à celle des modernes*, published in 1819. It was Constant who maintained that the liberty of the ancients was essentially a matter of citizenship; its economic basis was landownership, it glorified military prowess, and it was hostile to manual labour, an undignified activity which fell to slaves and non-citizens. It was in its way an attractive conception of freedom, but not for modern man. Ancient city-states existed in a condition of almost perpetual warfare, and no wonder when everyday life was so boring. Modern freedom was the quiet enjoyment of private life; its economic basis was inconsistent with slavery, for it demanded skilled labour, high productivity and a universal taste for prosperity. The liberty of the moderns might not appeal to nostalgic admirers of Rome and Sparta such as Machiavelli and Rousseau, but everyone now knew that when French Revolutionaries tried to reinvent the Roman Republic in late eighteenth-century Paris, they brought about mob rule, the Terror and Napoleon.[6]

Constant also pointed out something which is often overlooked: modern freedom might require more public spirit, more participation, and a more intelligent political public than its adherents supposed. Constant was not in the least an enthusiast for 'privatization', in the sense of a self-centred concern with one's own welfare to the exclusion of any larger concern. He did celebrate the pleasures of private life as well as the public life of the agora, and he was anxious to point out, *contra* Rousseau and other enthusiasts for turning back the clock, that the modern world was so much richer in pleasures than the ancient world that it was no loss to prefer it. In short, Constant suggests that the ancient world did not make a conscious choice in favour of ancient liberty; it was all it had. But we may in fact doubt whether the ancient tradition was as universally enthusiastic about participatory liberty as even Constant suggests.[7] Aristotle simply takes for granted the usual Greek view that holding office is a good which ought to be distributed according to justice; we all ought to have our due share of office-holding, because anything which people want and will quarrel over ought to be distributed on a basis they concur in thinking just. It is a modern view, much influenced by philosophical prejudice, that sees politics as creative and innovative, and the realm of the political as the realm in which one's personality was displayed on the public stage. The defence of politics as an arena for 'acting' which Hannah Arendt extracts from classical writers is not really there in the texts. Aristotle's politics is defensive, and not a script for psychodrama.[8]

It is not *political participation* as such which is the goal for Machiavelli, either, but a condition where ordinary people can get on with their lives unmolested by bandits in the guise of rulers. Certainly Machiavelli was awed by the military prowess of the Roman Republic and the glorious figure the Romans cut in history, but his praise of the way the Roman people participated in political life was instrumental. It was by simultaneously following the lead of their betters *and* keeping the arrogance of their betters in check that they preserved Roman freedom. That freedom was not the ascent from merely behaving to creatively acting which features in *The Human Condition*. Roman freedom had two aspects; externally it was a freedom from the power of other states and from the necessity to which weakness makes states subject; internally, it was freedom from the tyranny of the despot or the ambitious *grandi*. The property of the ordinary man was a sound basis for liberty because the ordinary man wished only to enjoy it in peace, whereas the 'grandi' were greedy and ambitious.

Machiavellian liberty is largely 'negative' liberty — freedom from various forms of oppression. It took Rousseau to characterize freedom as 'obedience to a law we prescribe to ourselves' — a characteristically modern and Calvinist thought — and attach it to his defence of the poor but virtuous ancient world against the rich but corrupt modern world. But Rousseau was true to the ancient tradition in wanting as little politics as possible; property, according to his essay on *Political Economy*, should enable each individual to live so far as possible without entanglements with others. It was not just a matter of keeping private interest in check, so that individuals would serve the public interest. It was, as in Plato's *Laws*, a matter of reducing the complexities and excitements of social and political life to a minimum.

If ancient liberty is more 'negative' and less 'participatory' than we might have thought, and the armed farmer a more defensive figure than many commentators suggest, modern liberty may itself be less negative. Not only Constant, but Mill and de Tocqueville held that negative liberty was threatened by mass society, and needed the support of something very like participatory democracy. De Tocqueville and Mill shared the 'negative' view that a major duty of the modern state was to guarantee the private rights of the individual subject, and so agreed that the subject's property was a main object of the subject's and therefore the state's concern. They all, especially de Tocqueville and Mill, feared that 'privatization' had gone too far, that the citizens of modern democracies were concerned only with their private possessions, and cared nothing for their larger liberties. They were all the more fearful because the threat to liberty that they feared came from the whole mass of the citizens. In essence, they feared that a complacent mass public would prefer comfort to progress, economic well-being to the pursuit of excellence, that they would become 'industrious sheep'. Their argument was much the same as the classical, Machiavellian argument that if the ruling class is to be checked, it can only be by a wide awake citizenry; but they faced a novel problem in the nineteenth-century context. This is that the ruling class which needs to be checked is the same as the citizen class which is to do the checking.[9]

What we find here is one vision of the threat to 'modern' liberty. In essence, one can usefully distinguish three views of

the dangers which threatened, and the remedies for them.
Some writers, Spencer and his successors among them, look to
a constitutional system which will so circumscribe government
and so entrench the rights of property that individual liberty in
the laissez-faire sense will be safe. The danger that threatens
liberty is misconceived benevolence, democratic demands for
redistribution, and attempts to create some form of welfare
state. Against this, the barrier to be erected is a firm constitution, backed by a consensus on the sanctity of property rights.
It is no accident that Robert Nozick's *Anarchy, State and
Utopia* is a condemnation of the usual American assumption
that a democratic government is self-evidently a legitimate
government.[10] In Nozick's view, liberty is a matter of the non-
infringement of rights, understood as 'holdings' in oneself
and other forms of property; we must insist on the illicitness of
any interference with those rights, whether by a majority or a
minority of one's fellows. To sceptics who question the theory
of natural rights, and enquire what rights we must entrench,
an alternative reply is that we ought by convention to establish
those rights and that conception of what rights amount to to
which the theory of natural rights is committed.[11] This view
still yields the connection between property and political freedom which Spencer sought. Individuals have as much freedom
as possible if and only if the range of decisions taken on the
basis of exchange between proprietors of material objects,
abilities and claims upon these is maximized, and coercive
decisions are confined to those operations of judiciary and
police required to enforce the rights of individuals. This is the
argument offered by von Hayek, who avowedly disbelieves in
natural rights, but defends something like Herbert Spencer's
minimal state.

Some writers who have shared this fear that property will
come under attack from a democratic pressure for redistribution and measures of public welfare, offer a different
perspective on the constitutional mechanisms of resistance.
The most famous statement of this view comes in James
Madison's *Federalist Paper, No. 10*. Madison says that many
people fear that the infant American republic will succumb to
party strife and factional conflict — an old fear in republican
thinking. There are only two ways of abolishing factions:
'one, by destroying the liberty which is essential to its

existence; the other, by giving to every citizen the same opinions, the same passions, and the same interests.' The first would be worse than the disease, the second is impracticable. Factions are inescapable. Still, we face the danger that in a pure democracy, the propertiless would bear down on the propertied, and would 'tyrannize' over them: 'Hence it is that such democracies have ever been spectacles of turbulence and contention; have ever been found incompatible with personal security or the rights of property; and have in general been as short in their lives as they have been violent in their deaths.'[12] Madison's remedy is the federal constitution of the United States; faction checks faction, interest checks interest. Citizen virtue is not over-stretched, but liberty and property are secure.

There is general agreement that Madison's belief in the virtues of federalism and a bi-cameral legislature was excessive. If there had ever been a 'majority faction' seriously intent on altering the constitution and so removing the barriers to its rule, nothing could have prevented it from doing so. As Robert Dahl has argued, it is the underlying diversity of interests and the continued political deference of the unpropertied many which has preserved the constitution, and thus the economic and legal order which Madison desired. It is less that the Madisonian remedy has worked than that it has never been called on.

A second view of the dangers facing modern liberty and the proper defences against those dangers is what we are offered by de Tocqueville and Mill. Neither thought that an insistence on the natural rights of the propertied could succeed; in just those conditions of social conflict where appeals to rights tend to be made, mankind is least likely to agree on what those rights are. The history of the past two centuries is the history of the rise of democracy, and it is no use supposing that the power of the majority will be held up by waving the theory of natural rights at the masses. De Tocqueville feared that modern property privatized its owners; Mill denounced America as a country in which 'they have the six points of Chartism, and they have no poverty, and all that these advantages do for them is that the life of the whole of one sex is devoted to dollar-hunting and of the other to breeding dollar hunters'.[13] The middle-class — not proletarian — democracy which resulted would be uniformitarian, resentful of dissent. The result would not be tyranny in a violent form, but 'a tyranny of opinion' and an end to individuality and innovation.

Mill and de Tocqueville both had a conception of liberty which will not fit neatly into the categories of positive or negative liberty. It was certainly both positive and negative. One might say that they wanted the maximum of negative liberty and a minimum of government direction in order that individuals should launch out into freely chosen lives of their own. De Tocqueville's eyes were as much on France as America; he feared that the French history of centralization and a bureaucratic state would give all power to the numerical majority. Such a condition could well be comfortable, but it would be stifling. Neither Mill nor de Tocqueville remotely considered the possibility of a democratic dictatorship — that is, of a dictator claiming and perhaps having mass backing — of the sort to which the twentieth-century has become accustomed. Hitler and Stalin were outside their imaginative range. None the less, both understood very well that privatized individuals would not be a secure barrier against would-be despots; the French peasantry helped Napoleon III to power, and the French peasantry were a by-word for obsessive clutching at their own patch of land and their own property. American prosperity, American decentralization, the scale of the country and the open frontier all combatted the dangers of democratic tyranny; European countries had to find their own remedies.

De Tocqueville relied very heavily on decentralization. More interestingly for our purposes, Mill turned to a form of socialism, or perhaps one ought to say, to a form of economic democracy. Since property was the creature of law, not a matter of natural right, governments might rearrange the legal and economic arrangements of their society as they thought fit. It was no use for the capitalist owners of industry to denounce this as the destruction of liberty; most workers had no more liberty to choose their occupation than slaves had had, and anyone who worked for wages spent his working life taking orders. The property of the owners of capital gave them power over those who had to sell their labour, and it was right to ask whether this was not itself a threat to freedom.[14] Worker-owned and managed cooperatives would both teach the working class the kind of self-restraint and 'long-termism' which democracy demanded, and be themselves a contribution to freedom. The freedom would be distinctively 'modern' — a cooperative economy would be decentralized, competitive and largely laissez-faire, and the moral ideals of such a society would be individualist and innovative. The property forms would self-evidently be so too. It will not have escaped the reader's notice that this kind of argument has come back to citizen virtue after all; and in the process we come back to the place of those considerations which in an earlier age were arguments for small independent freeholding farmers, and for substantial economic equality — or, perhaps it would be less misleading to say, for an economic system which curtailed the possibility of amassing very great wealth, and saw to it that nobody fell into dependence through destitution. Mill's view was that the working class would demand and would have to have economic citizenship: 'I cannot think that they will be permanently contented with the condition of labouring for wages as their ultimate state. They may be willing to pass through the class of servants on their way to that of employers, but not to remain in it all their lives.'[15]

The nineteenth-century saw an agonized argument over this; Sir Henry Maine, whose *Ancient Law* had traced the origins of modern law back to its origins in the communities which predated the classical world, had summarized the process in the famous slogan 'from status to contract'.[16] He was much less hostile to the privatized present than Mill and de Tocqueville, much less optimistic about improving democracy by extending it. The modern world was one of independent individuals, encountering one another through contractual relationships; they and their property alike had been liberated from customary ties which would have slotted them without appeal into stable hierarchies and fixed traditional ways of life. The rise of democracy threatens to take us back down the path up which we have struggled. If the labouring classes have the vote, they will recreate the dependency of property on politics which the ancient world displayed. So, it is vital to stand out against democracy.

Mill thought this was about as plausible as trying to turn back the tide. In this he was surely right, even though as a prophet of the democratic future he comes off badly, for he was doubly unrealistic in thinking that mankind would shortly refuse to defer to wealth but could readily be taught to defer to superior intelligence and merit.[17] Mill thought that self-reliance was so satisfying that a self-reliant working class would be unlikely to fetter the better off, and unlikely to fall into the sort of poverty which would tempt them to do so. If the working class was emancipated from wage slavery, and became self-employing and self-managing, the citizenship qualities needed if democracy and liberalism were to be compatible can be achieved. What Mill's argument shows is that a concern with the bases of freedom in the free use of property and in government non-intervention can be detached from an obsession with individual private property as usually understood, while individual freedom remains the standard by which political success and failure are to be judged.

The case remains firmly within the political tradition of arguments over property. It shifts its ground, of course, because it no longer looks for salvation to self-subsistent farmers, and its vision of the free republic is no longer that of Harrington's *Oceana*. Yet it still connects the idea of 'the middle people' of Bacon and Harrington with a society which protects individual liberty against tyrannical government. Mill, like de Tocqueville, thought it necessary to defend liberty on moral and psychological grounds, too; the essay on *Liberty* appeals to all manner of considerations about the attractions of individuality and the search for individual excellence, against an explicit background of anxiety about the liberticide possibilities of democracy in a mass society.[18]

Mill's reformist liberalism by no means ended the debate. On the contrary, it always strikes laissez-faire liberals as excessively tender to socialism and socialists dismiss it as altogether too half-hearted. A third vision of the threats to modern liberty and the answer to those threats is offered by recent theorists of the welfare state. The threat to modern liberty is essentially the proletarianization of the worker. It is not so much that democratic demands for security and comfort will destroy liberty as that an uncontrolled search for private gain will shut large numbers out of the advantages of the developed modern economic order. The resulting proletariat may be recruited by extremist movements and destroy liberty in that way: this is the fear of the theorists of 'mass society'.[19] More usually, the objection is that the proletariat is shut out from the life of its own society. It is little better than a slave class, on which rests the society which gives it nothing in return. Property ought to promote freedom twice over; it must give individuals access to the life of their society, which is a matter of increasing freedom of choice rather than simply increasing their welfare; and in the process it must make them more able to bear the inevitable failures and disappointments of political life without succumbing to the urge to destroy the system they live under. The connection with ownership in the narrowest sense is indirect; it is not a matter of securing any particular sort of property to everyone, so much as securing access to whatever promotes a self-confident sense of equal citizenship. Yet it allows a defence of the 'welfare state' which is political in that it is not tied to the provision of welfare in the sense of food, clothes and shelter, so much as to 'enabling goods', those goods which allow their possessors to choose for themselves what life plans to try to implement. So, in such a perspective, we find that education is generally reckoned a crucial element in welfare state provision, not for the paternalist reason that education is a 'merit good', that is something which everyone ought to have, nor just because more education now leads to more income later, but rather because it enables its possessors to carve out their own paths in the world.[20]

Energetic libertarians who start from the natural rights perspective would retort that enablements of this kind cannot be secured by what amounts to theft from the 'holdings' of others.[21] That is why the argument has recently turned once again on the question — discussed at some length in Part Two — whether property is held by something like natural right or social convention. The welfare state liberalism just described is what we find defended in John Rawls's *Theory of Justice*. This starts in a 'rights-less' universe, but in a moral framework in which individual self-respect is one of the central goods, and asks what political and economic rights we must grant one another. Conversely, when Robert Nozick tries to demolish this conception of what justice demands, he has to argue that rights are prior to any social contract and are proprietary in nature.[22]

If we side with Rawls, there is an instrumental question of a serious and contentious kind to be answered before we can defend the welfare state as advancing citizenship as well as welfare. This is whether property rights can be so designed that whatever transfers from the better off to the worse off are required to secure the freedom of manoeuvre for the less well endowed do not diminish liberty more than they enhance it. Even if we do not accept Nozick's view that individual 'holdings' are so sacrosanct that they cannot be touched for such purposes, and that a concern for liberty can be displayed only by 'hands off', we may well have qualms about how much government intervention to swallow before drawing the line on libertarian grounds.[23]

In the past two centuries various answers have been given. One was popular with the Idealists from Hegel through to T.H. Green and his successors in late nineteenth-century England. This depended on an interpretation of liberty as the expression of a developed personality, attached to its social setting and its moral convictions, a moral perspective we shall see more of in Part Two. Personal rights, such as the right to personal security, religious toleration, a free choice of career and so on were basic and sacred. They and the rights of ownership had one thing in common, which is that they rested on a presumption that humanity had authority over material nature — freedom of speech presupposes the right to employ my mouth to make noises, though more besides of course, the right to life entails that I may eat plants and fruits, the right to ownership entails that I may exercise sovereignty over mere physical things. (As we shall see, one of Marx's objections to the regime of capitalist private property rested on taking Hegel seriously; 'ownership' failed to give men power over things and ended by giving things power over men.) The Idealist tradition thought that the anarchy of the market could be controlled, and that by a judicious mixture of government intervention and individual, market-oriented behaviour, individual and social personality could be fully expressed. Unregulated capitalism embodied pure self-assertion on the part of the capitalist, along with something not far short of slavery for the proletarian, and therefore had little to be said for it, while a semi-socialized economy in which ownership was understood as a social function might properly express a socialized self. This view appears in R.H. Tawney's essay on *The Acquisitive Society* as well as in T.H. Green's much earlier reflections on freedom of contract. It is an answer to the problem we posed above in that it does not suggest that complete socialization is desirable; individual initiative and a modicum of independence is needed, but if the strong run amok the weak will perish.[24] T.H. Marshall's *Class and Citizenship* applies the thought to the welfare state of the 1950s.

John Rawls's *Theory of Justice* suggests another way of reaching the same end. Initially, Rawls offers a strongly 'negative' view of freedom as non-interference; the maintenance of freedom is thus to be discussed separately from economic questions, for the latter are about welfare rather than liberty. Rawls introduces the notion of 'primary goods', however, those goods which one needs in order to lead a self-respecting existence, no matter what one's particular goals turn out to be; he ties this conception of primary goods to a concern for an equality of self-respect. It now appears that primary goods are goods which enable us to make something of our lives; but such 'enablements' as we might call them are only fully at home in a more positive and participatory conception of liberty. Rawls himself hesitates between a rigid insistence that (negative) liberty may never be sacrificed to welfare and a more flexible doctrine that the *value* of liberty to the poorly endowed is so diminished that they must be brought up to a tolerable level of capacity even at the cost of some liberty. The result, though it is inelegantly achieved, is persuasive. Political liberty is sacred, and so is moral liberty, but the correct mixture of private ownership and public control is open to judicious adjustment. Enthusiasts for positive liberty will think that they could reach the same goal more swiftly: property is to be judged as an aid to widespread self-government; it is implausible to suppose that unregulated capitalism or state socialism are the best we can do. On this point, J.S. Mill, John Rawls and many others would unite.[25]

It remains to tie this concern into the traditional concern for stability and good citizenship, and to show how antique concerns are not of merely antiquarian interest. The vision of the social democratic polity into which this — as opposed to the Harringtonian or Machiavellian — concern for the good citizen and the free republic has to fit is distinctively modern. It refuses to shut out women, manual workers and the unpropertied from 'citizenship'. It separates citizenship from

military prowess and the ownership of arms. Its vision of the
free republic is not one in which the maintenance of an army
and its employment in colonization is a major concern. Yet it
depends on the thought that citizens must have adequate
inducements to be loyal to their society, and it sees the
same need for stable livelihoods and stable social relationships.

We must, of course, recognize that the old recipe is hid-
eously implausible — small farmers are driven out of business
by the rise of agro-business, and turn to extremists, usually of
the right but occasionally of the left; small shopkeepers are in
the same plight. The old belief that 'moderate property leads
to moderate ambitions leads to moderate politics' is destroyed
by the impact of industrialization, and the increased scale
of the modern economy. The middle ranks on whom everyone
relied for social stability until the end of the nineteenth-
century now frighten democratic theorists to death. There is
good reason for this, though the literature is oddly silent on
the subject. Property is as much a source of anxiety as it is of
security. It is one thing to own a piece of ground which will
provide enough and a little over for yourself and your
family — that is security. It is quite another when that piece
of ground has to be devoted to cash crops which may fail to
sell in a given season and so leave you and your family
destitute — that is anxiety. The property of many of the
middling sort has become the second rather than the first. It is
no wonder that these are the supporters of extreme conservative movements; the violence of their fears renders them
vulnerable to such appeals, and their hankering after security
drives them to the right of the political spectrum. We know
that security rather than property is what we are after; but we
also know that we do not want to sacrifice everything else to
it. What we cannot claim is that we know vastly more than our
predecessors about how to achieve it. Job security, sometimes
described as 'new property' by social theorists, is an obvious
point at which to apply the old insights; individuals who feel
that their own futures are tolerably secure are better able to see
their own society as a guarantor of their security, and to see
themselves as duty bound to do their part in keeping it going.
Modest state intervention to ensure that security is exactly in
line with Rousseau's plea that those who laid down the rules of

mine and thine should see to it that everyone who was willing to work should be able to support himself and his family. It cannot now be achieved by settling everyone on a small-holding; it does not follow that the task is less important than Rousseau thought.

PART TWO:

DEFENCES OF

PRIVATE PROPERTY

There is no one way of distinguishing defences and criticisms of private property. A plausible way, and one adopted here, is to distinguish defences based on utility, natural rights, the promotion of personality and the defence of liberty. The political aspect of this last defence we have seen already. They inevitably run into each other; a utilitarian who believes that freedom is a major component of happiness will readily accept that property ought to promote freedom; so equally will a 'personalist' who thinks that the ability to act freely is a central element of personality. Many accounts of natural rights derive them from God's concern for human happiness, and may thus derive the right to use and appropriate from a prior right to life and the pursuit of happiness. If they are thus able to import and incorporate aspects of each other's arguments, they remain analytically distinct, and their fundamental allegiances quite unlike one another.

4
Utility and Property

The simplest defence of the existence of property rights over external objects is directly utilitarian. Unless individuals had the right to appropriate, use, transfer and (perhaps) bequeath objects of value or interest, it would be impossible to use the raw materials provided by nature for anything other than the simplest sort of immediate consumption. The creation of such rights is, therefore, dictated by utility.[1] Utilitarianism is a normative theory which holds that moral and legal rules are acceptable to the extent that their acceptance and enforcement promote happiness. It is hostile to doctrines of 'natural right', holding that legal rights must be a matter of positive law, and that 'moral rights' are explicable as liberties and powers which individuals *ought* to have in order to promote their most important interests. Although property rights are not the dictates of 'nature', what one might call the moral shadow of ownership — a presumption that an individual who has harmlessly acquired an object ought to be able to enjoy it undisturbed — is readily derived from utilitarian considerations, such as the thought that individuals have a right to security and autonomy, because the possession and enforcement of such a right is 'optimific'.[2]

Characteristically, utilitarians have so taken for granted this simple moral point that they have been more anxious to insist on the difference between a simple moral presumption in favour of unmolested possession, and property rights in their full-fledged form. These latter are necessarily the creatures of the law.[3] It is the question, 'what property rights ought the law to create and enforce?' that utilitarianism most naturally raises and most distinctively answers. Unsurprisingly, utilitarians have directed their attention to ownership as it is understood in modern European legal systems.

Ownership under a developed legal system has been well

characterized by A.M. Honoré along the following lines: 'Ownership comprises the right to possess, the right to use, the right to manage, the right to the income of the thing, the right to the capital, the right to security, the rights or incidents of transmissibility and absence of term, the prohibition of harmful use, liability to execution, and the incident of residuarity: this makes eleven leading incidents.'[4] It is to be noticed that our loose way of speaking of property as 'a bundle of rights' is inadequate to the extent that it excludes liability to execution — that is the vulnerability of property to being seized and sold in payment of one's debts; the notion of a bundle of *rights* also excludes probibition of harmful use, but one might demur at including this as an incident of ownership without further ado. I am prohibited from using *anyone's* knife to stab you in the chest, so many harmful uses are prohibited without reference to ownership, whereas liability to execution is very much part of ownership. What attaches to ownership is less the prohibition of harmful use than liability for injuries *caused by* my property in the absence of human criminality — if a slate blows off the roof of my house and strikes you it is to me you will look for compensation. One might say that the price of sovereignty over one's possessions is responsibility for their misdeeds.[5]

A legal order recognizes ownership in the full modern sense when all these rights and duties are assigned to a single person. If they are split up and assigned to different people, or if some do not exist at all, it is a pre- or post-modern system. Simple societies often treat the community or the extended family as the bearer of the right of residuarity — that is, when all lesser rights have lapsed, the object returns to the family rather than to a particular individual; the communist society of the future envisaged by Marx will not have the same notion of rights as ourselves, but will certainly spread these incidents over several persons and institutions. The utilitarian defence of property in any form is thus the defence of the legal recognition of ownership as an instrument in promoting the greatest happiness. The defence of exactly this conception of ownership is a defence of attaching all these incidents to one person; a utilitarian critique of this conception condemns these arrangements as less than optimific. It has been suggested that it makes no sense to ask whether ownership ought to be recognized; if ownership is defined as *all* relations between persons with respect to things, then there is something to be said for the view that all societies must have some use for ownership, and the only question is what sort of ownership they ought to recognize.[6] But it is an exaggeration. Persons could relate to one another with respect to things without ownership entering into the matter. The hunters who allow the man who kills the beast they chase to take the first piece of meat from it neither claim ownership of the beast for themselves nor confer it on the successful hunter. It is analytically more sensible to distinguish claims made to ownership or on the basis of ownership from all other claims on things. You may have good reason to use my bicycle, perhaps that you are in a hurry to perform some good; but your relation to me over the bicycle is not a matter of ownership, whereas my having the right to accept or reject your claims to its use is a matter of ownership.

We shall see in Part Three that what is commonly called the economic theory of property rights makes the twin claims that in order to put any resource to best use, it is optimific to make sure that somebody owns it in the full liberal sense, and that the legal recognition of property rights has evolved under the impulse of pressures towards efficiency through a process parallel to that of natural selection. Here, however, we must concentrate on the main outlines of the utilitarian theory itself. The background assumptions of the utilitarian defence of property are that nature is niggardly, men demanding, labour disagreeable, and anxiety even worse.[7] We thus need to devise ways of making nature yield as much as she can, with the minimum expenditure of effort; we cannot do without rules of mine and thine because most men are of limited altruism and some will try to take the fruits of another man's efforts if they are not prevented. And even if men were not disposed to try to seize the results of other men's efforts, property rights would still be useful because of the way they solve problems of coordination between cooperators. If you and I know who has what claims over the various factors that would have to go into making some novel useful object, we can organize its creation because we can decide who is to have what share of the benefits it yields, and know whose say-so is decisive in allowing us to employ the various factors which enter into making it.

Property satisfies the need for security, and allows the

natural incentive to labour to succeed — we are impelled to labour by the mere desire to stay alive, but no man will sow where another may reap in his stead; by guaranteeing that we may call our own our own, rules of ownership ensure that our desire for well-being will lead us to work.[8] Equally, the enforcement of freely made contracts serves the same ends; if I have what will do you more good than it does me and you have what will do me more good than it does you, exchange is the way forward. Direct barter is clumsy, and that indicates the need for money. Money is what Marx termed 'the universal equivalent', allowing the utility of exchange to be realized without needless physical movement of goods.[9]

The argument runs swiftly and smoothly. What it does not do is distinguish very readily between the need for *property* and the need for *private* property. Would utility be best served by, for instance, leaving the right to the capital in the hands of families and only the income in the hands of particular individuals? There is no difficulty in effecting something analogous when an estate descends by will; it is not uncommon for the widow or widower to receive an income for life while the capital itself belongs to her or his children. Would it be intolerably cumbersome if individuals had to secure family assent to plans for investment? It probably would be, so if we think economic growth more important than family authority, we shall think the modern system of ownership superior to its rivals. If we think the side-effects of leaving investment decisions in private hands are excessively disagreeable in various ways — environmentally intolerable, prone to lead to massive concentrations of economic power in too few hands, or whatever — we may look for non-ownership based ways of controlling them, or for forms of social ownership which will secure such control while remaining more flexible and less lethargic than pre-modern family ownership.[10] The question is always the same: what system of ownership would be optimific? The response will therefore vary according to our sociological hunches about the side-effects of different allocations of rights, as well as according to our views about what contributes most to human happiness.

In the same spirit, we may ask whether it is the best possible arrangement to allow ownership to be 'without term' where entities like land are concerned. Perhaps land generally, or some land in particular, ought only to be held on something like a leasehold, the land reverting to the community or some body representing the community, after that time. What if we faced a new territory which we hoped to see occupied and cultivated? We might think that one possibility was to allow people to acquire any amount of land so long as they could bring it under cultivation, and to grant them a shorthold, of, say, a dozen years, at the end of which time they might simply hand it back, and use their savings to buy some smaller quantity outright, or be required to sell it back at some settled price. Why might we do this? If we wished to spread the ownership of land around the population, but wanted to get as much into cultivation as possible and as fast as possible, we might think this route better than allowing unlimited or limited freehold acquisition.

The argument in favour of something nearer our own system of indeterminate ownership is that it allows us to buy and sell a clearer and less encumbered title. If the law permits a single person, so to speak, to collect all the incidents of ownership in his or her hands, then individuals may, as the French Code puts it, deal with things in the most absolute manner permitted by the law. Moreover, this will permit the owner to erect all sorts of subsidiary rights on top of his ownership. The owner who can raise a loan on the security of his land may if he is rational and efficient employ the money so raised to increase his income well beyond what is needed to repay the loan.[11] It evidently promotes the general happiness that he should be able to do so; the law therefore ought to recognize mortgages. But only if the owner's powers of disposal of the land are complete will the prospective lender be happy with the security offered; so we have here an argument for unencumbered, non-determining ownership from which lesser interests may be carved.

The argument needs many further refinements before it becomes persuasive. For instance, nothing has yet been said about the range of things that can become the object of ownership. In many societies, men have been able to own slaves, and in many others, offices such as judgeships or military commissions have been bought and sold. Some writers, for instance Hegel, have suggested that there is some sort of logical contradiction in the idea that such things can be owned. Ownership, they say, is ownership of *things*, objects which have no wills of their own; to claim to own a person is absurd, because persons are by definition beings with wills and perspectives of their own, subjects not objects.[12] Ownership of offices is not absurd in the same way, but is none the less irrational. The essence of an office is public service and the logic of access to it is competence in doing that office's duties. Purchase assimilates it to what is properly bought and sold at will, and used without inhibition for the owner's own good.[13]

The utilitarian cannot accept such an outlook. Property is the creature of the law, and if the law creates slaves and creates property rights in offices, then people just do own slaves and colonelcies. The argument against such forms of property is not that there is something conceptually amiss, but that they are condemned by the principle of utility. Slavery is very much disliked by slaves; even where slaves are well-fed, comfortable and even the possessors of great power — under the Roman Empire some slaves became what later ages would have described as senior civil servants — no free man would change places with them.[14] There is thus a strong prima facie case against slavery. Strong though it is, it can be overridden; Mill thought ancient society could have taken no steps forward without the existence of slavery, and was half-inclined to justify it on such (Aristotelian) terms. But in the modern world it would plainly be intolerable.[15] It is, so to speak, a bonus for utilitarian criticisms of slavery that slavery is also an inefficient way of organizing production. Free labour has always been much more efficient.[16]

What is noticeable about the utilitarian condemnation of slavery, however, is what it leaves out; utilitarians cannot simply denounce slavery as a violation of human rights or of a man's 'property in his own person' in the way natural rights theorists can.[17] It is not that slavery is only 'extrinsically' bad, for it is quite clear that it is in itself a miserable condition; rather, its intrinsic badness can in principle, though only rarely in practice, be overridden by a sufficient addition to human happiness, a claim that believers in natural rights cannot accept.

The case against property in government offices or military ranks is less contentious. It simply appeals to the evident inefficiency of a method of recruitment which depends on ability to pay rather than on some objective test of capacity. The flexibility of utilitarian arguments on this sort of issue is very considerable; we may consider the effects of changing from purchase to appointment on merit in terms of its effect on morale, or on 'raw' efficiency of performance; we may consider the questions of how far the holders of these abusive forms of property are entitled to compensation, balancing the need to preserve the security of property rights and justice between owners against the need to abolish abuses at a reasonable price. Even in the case of the abolition of slavery, the least defensible of all forms of ownership, the utilitarian may — and nineteenth-century utilitarians did — argue that the individual slave-owner had aquired a piece of property legitimate at the time, and should therefore be compensated for being expropriated.[18]

It is characteristic of utilitarian arguments that they are reversible; that is, since all justification rests on a consideration of consequences, a reconsideration of consequences will force a reconsideration of what is being justified. Moreover the malleability of human reactions allows utilitarians to ask whether the attitudes whose gratification or frustration determines how much happiness an institution produces are more or less the effects of the institution in question. Expectations are crucial in utilitarian arguments over property rights. Gratified expectation is a great source of happiness; property is founded in and gives rise to expectation. It is thus capable of giving great happiness and it can be a source of great misery if expectations are frustrated. So it is important to know whether expectations can be reshaped or attached to new entities without too much trouble. We may often be optimistic. Thus, a colonel who is looking forward to passing on his colonelcy to his son gets pleasure from the expectation, but he might get even more pleasure from the knowledge that his son's promotion was due to his merits. Again, the particular pleasure we get from thinking of our property in the hands of our children may attach just as readily to the house he can buy with the compensation he gets when he is 'bought out' as it now does to the colonelcy.

Utilitarian arguments provide good, but lukewarm defences of private property, and by the same token provide good but lukewarm defences of public ownership, too.[19] Since property rights are to be justified in terms of general benefit, due attention being paid to the importance of individual security and freedom of thought and action, the ownership of anything beyond consumer goods and the like is a matter of convenience; moreover, given the 'bundle of rights and liabilities' conception of ownership, utilitarians are happy to envisage ownership being broken up, so that control over the capital may be separated from the right to income, and residuary rights be detached from current control. This is anticipated in the complicated arrangements which underpin leasehold ownership of residential property in England and Wales, and in the relations of shareholders to the companies they own but by no means control.[20] The utilitarian cannot accommodate Hegel's thought that the human will is essentially individual and property therefore essentially private property, nor the Marxian counter that production is essentially social and property therefore essentially social and all pre-communist societies an aberration sustained by brute force and ideological deception. Property may be more or less private or more or less public; there is only one question worth asking — 'what rights over the resources for production and consumption ought we to recognize, and in whose hands should we vest them?'

Natural Rights and Natural Owners

The utilitarian's approach to property rights builds up a conception of ownership out of other rights not essentially connected with property. Some natural rights theorists by contrast derive all rights from a conception of property as 'self-ownership'.[1] Since this is not true of all natural rights theorists, this section unavoidably tackles its subject matter in two bites, first by showing how a non-property conception of rights tackles the defence of property rights, then by showing the consequences of a more property-like conception of rights.

The traditional theory of natural rights (insofar as it was one entity) characteristically derived individual rights from the law of God, or Nature or Reason. The American Declaration of Independence announced that its framers held 'these truths to be self-evident, that all men are endowed by their Creator with certain inalienable Rights, that among these are Life, Liberty and the pursuit of Happiness. To secure these rights, Governments are instituted among Men, deriving their just powers from the consent of the governed . . . .'[2] Parallel claims were made in the French Declaration of the Rights of Man and of Citizens. In many, the natural rights included a natural right *to* property: article II of the French Declaration of 1791 holds that 'The end of all political associations, is the preservation of the natural and imprescriptible rights of man; and these rights are liberty, property, security, and resistance of oppression.'[3] Similar claims are made in the Virginia Declaration which was in most respects a model for the Declaration of Independence.

The question arises, what was the natural right to property a right to do or to have, and scarcely less urgently, what elements of the traditional claim can survive a more sceptical and more secular age, which finds it implausible to talk of the dictates of God, Nature and Reason? Happily, answering the first question will take us some way to the answer to the second. Natural rights were held to be natural in virtue of their historical or moral precedence over legal rights; governments were legitimate insofar as they bent their efforts to protect our natural rights, illegitimate if they violated them. Moreover, the doctrine differed from utilitarianism in being strikingly individualistic; each of us is obliged to obey the government so long as it upholds our natural rights, but if it violates them, we are under no further obligation to obey. Even if the violation could be justified on utilitarian grounds, we are not obliged to obey.[4] Rights set limits to what governments may do, as well as setting them the positive task of protecting each of us against violations of our rights.

The right to property, however, is less easy to analyse than the right to life, liberty and security. These are easy to analyse, in that they translate readily into the thought that other persons have a duty *not* to kill, enslave or endanger us; governments exist to make sure other people perform that negative duty. What about the right to property? Is it amenable to the same analysis? On the face of it, it seems difficult to apply it. Suppose we include the right of bequest in the idea of property; I need more than mere abstention from interference if I am to make a successful bequest. If my desire to pass on my property to my daughter is to be satisfied, I need the positive, posthumous assistance of trustees, lawyers and courts. To put the same point another way round, although it is evident that my rights over my property do impose duties of abstention on others — you must *not* steal it, damage it, or use it without my permission — this tells us nothing about how far the natural right of ownership extends.[5]

In the traditional literature, there are many suggestions and many more inexplicit assumptions. For simplicity's sake, we may take two extreme suggestions about the extent of ownership, before considering how natural rights theories have to treat the other crucial question, 'what can we have property rights in?' One extreme suggestion would hold that 'natural right' only covers the right to the undisturbed and harmless uses of things in their natural state, all else being social convention.[6] The other extreme suggestion would hold that acquisition in the state of nature gives the possessor a freehold interest of the sort recognized by modern legal systems.[7] The first suggestion rests on the obvious fact that we must take and consume what the world offers if we are to live at all; we could hardly have a natural right to life but no right to use what is in the environment to preserve ourselves. Indeed, in the writings of Locke we are told that we are enjoined by God to preserve ourselves, so we have a duty as well as a right to do so.[8] Others, therefore, possessing the same rights as we do, may, like us, take and consume the bounty of nature; save in self-defence we may not interfere with their doing so. What may count as self-defence is itself implied by the theory of natural right; if a man puts up a fence with the intention of thereby starving me, this is an assault, and I may resist. If he gathers only six apples from a tree and leaves dozens of equally good ones, I may not covet the ones he has picked, but must get others for myself.

The argument hinges on a buried utilitarian assumption about the point of such rights, but is none the less an argument about what *each* person may do in the exercise of their individual rights. For generations, the complications have been seen to lie at the next stage of the argument. Even where we are gathering nature's bounty, some things will not be immediately consumed; fruit and nuts and scoops of water will be, but the simple hut of branches and mud will not be. The argument will, however, plausibly stretch to cover it. Harmless use is not to be interfered with; so long as I manifest the clear intention to use and occupy my hut, it remains mine.[9] How much further can we go? On the face of it, we can advance step by step quite a long way. If I prefer your hut to mine and we exchange, it seems that we do nobody any harm and may therefore each occupy our new huts on the same terms as before. What if I turn out to be good at hut-building and bad at hunting deer; may we exchange deer for huts? Readers of Adam Smith will recognize all this as a version of the 'rude state of society' which he set out as a model by which to clear our ideas about trade and the terms of trade.[10]

Those unacquainted with Smith will see that it is in effect an argument about how far we can stretch the thought that arrangements made with full and free consent could build up

towards the modern conception of ownership on the foundation of 'non-interference with harmless uses'. The sticking
point comes where other people begin to claim that a given use
is not harmless. Some cases seem simple; if the river is high,
my bathing pool does no harm, but if it is low, my dam must
come down because it cuts off your drinking water. Some are
contentious; if you make even better huts than I and you offer
to make them for the person who supplies my deer, is your
trading harmful to me and therefore a prohibited use? It certainly damages me, and it is no use saying that I have no right
to complain of damage caused by the way you use your property, because in the terms of *this* argument (as opposed to the
one we shall shortly consider), 'property' is parasitic on harm-
lessness; we are not tailoring the concept of harm to fit that of
property.[11]

To cut a long story short, it would appear that a theory of
natural rights which begins in this minimal way, will have to
regard the eleborated property rights of a developed legal
system as essentially conventional. If they are, then they must
be instrumentally judged; they must serve the ends of all legal
conventions, namely the preservation of our natural rights,
and they must be created and maintained by means which also
respect our natural rights. Thus, we find all Declarations
setting great store by rules forbidding arbitrary and uncom-
pensated appropriation by governments, rules requiring a
legal backing for all taxation, and so on. We do not find any
suggestion that complete laissez-faire is a dictate of the law of
nature; what we find is that governments are bound to establish laws regulating property in due form, and are then bound
to observe them.[12]

This minimalist view with its concomitant instrumentalism
about developed legal rights issues naturally in the ideas of
contemporary writers such as Rawls and Dworkin. Given an
attachment to 'rights as trumps' or to the thought that a
theory of rights reflects the need for society to guarantee
a sphere within which the individual is inviolable and
invulnerable to even the well-meaning utilitarian calculations
of government, we speedily see that governments must establish private property in what one might call the goods of final
consumption, for they are essential to our having any individuality at all; equally, we must have free access to different

occupations. What does not follow is that one system of ownership is uniquely fitted to safeguard our rights.[13] Public or private ownership of productive enterprises is a matter of public prudence; if it is simpler to run a capitalist, private-ownership based economy, we should do so, and if not, not. If private ownership creates pockets of economic power which make it harder to secure individual freedom and a respect for civil rights, we would be justified in curtailing private ownership; if public ownership was excessively hard to square with open access to occupations, we should be justified in turning away from public ownership. The argument is like the utilitarian arguments we have just considered in being instrumental, unlike them in considering questions of property as instrumental in the protection of individual *rights* as well as in the creation of material *welfare*.

This approach is not the only possible approach within a natural right perspective. The other extreme starts from a proprietary conception of rights and advances at once to individualized private property. Grotius in the seventeenth-century and Robert Nozick in the last decade, for instance, hold that the 'natural right to property' implies that when we acquire something over which others have no prior right of ownership we get an outright freehold in it.[14] The intuitive plausibility of this is obvious; if I pick up a nugget of gold on some unoccupied shore, whose is it, if not mine? It was nobody's before I got there, and I have now taken it into my ownership. What this amounts to is my claiming the right to do with it whatever I choose, so long as I do not violate anyone else's rights in the process. I may do with it what anyone may lawfully do with anything; but I cannot claim that since the nugget is mine, I may beat you on the head with it.[15]

From here to fully-fledged property in the modern sense is a very short step; since I am sovereign over the object thus acquired I may make whatever deals I choose with anyone else. Third parties whose position is rendered less eligible by these deals cannot complain unless these deals are designed to prevent them using their own resources in the same way we are using ours. If you use your superior skills as a hut-maker, or exploit your access to superior branches, you do not 'harm' me in the sense in which 'harming others' is here meant. Our natural right to make free use of whatever we legitimately possess or acquire is not infringed by the competition of others, whatever the impact on our welfare.

This doctrine very obviously favours private property. The natural acquirers are individuals, and the relationship between them and their possessions is the relationship with which we are familiar from a developed legal system. Whether anyone is legitimately the owner of whatever he or she claims to own is a question of history; if he or she acquired it, either directly from the stock of unowned things about him or her, or else by a series of exchanges between legitimate owners, then their ownership is unimpugnable.[16] It does not rule out social or public ownership absolutely, but it does insist that the only legitimate route to its institution is via unanimous agreement to it. If we decide to contribute our existing holdings in order to create a socialist society, that is our business; but it would be a violation of our natural rights if anyone were to confiscate our property for the purpose.

The plausibility of this view of the matter can be properly assessed only after we look at the idea that all rights are proprietary. Before we consider its plausibility, we should also consider the way in which natural rights theories answer the question of what objects we may properly own. Evidently, all sides agree that objects of immediate use are ownable. Equally, things which are consumable over a longer run are ownable. Whether land is ownable outright by the mere right of nature is more contentious; Rousseau and Thomas Paine had their doubts, and one might think that John Rawls and Ronald Dworkin cast doubt upon it too.[17] Certainly, such freehold ownership can be 'trumped' by considerations based on personal rights.

What seems ruled out at once is slavery. If we are born free and equal, slavery cannot be accepted, since the person who is born a slave is born to be a mere object, part of the estate of another. Historically, in fact, natural rights theorists have taken various routes to legitimate slavery. The Kentucky Constitution of 1850 declared that 'The right of property is before and higher than any constitutional sanction, and the right of the owner of a slave to such slave and its increase is the same as the right of the owner of any property whatever.'[18] It remained unrepealed many years after the Civil War. In fact, there is nothing very surprising about most natural rights justifications of slavery. There are two routes by which it can be achieved. The first is to observe that slavery is a proper punishment for gross breaches of natural law; Locke suggested that captives taken in a just war, who might without injustice be killed, may be offered their lives on servile terms.[19] It goes without saying that this cannot justify hereditary servitude. The other is to rest current servitude on initial freedom; if I may dispose of whatever I have rights over, I may sell myself into slavery. Grotius explicitly claimed this, and it is an implication of Robert Nozick's theory. Grotius, however, thought it implied servitude for my descendants, while Nozick's theory, though silent on the whole subject, plainly implies that it does not.[20]

We can see, therefore, that natural rights theories make life difficult for slavery in a different fashion from utilitarianism. Because utilitarianism is a theory which looks to the aggregate happiness, it has nothing much to say about the allocation of property to individuals, and by the same token nothing much to say about who ought to be a slave if anyone ought to be. We might integrate considerations of justice or notions of personal right into a utilitarian theory by claiming, let us say, that a system of slavery would be intolerable if people expected to be enslaved on any other terms than as a punishment for very grave crimes.[21] According to the ingenuity of the argument, we might think of ourselves as constraining the pursuit of happiness by demanding a concern for justice and desert, or we might think that we could show that a really sophisticated utilitarianism would accommodate those considerations too. Natural rights theories would rule out slavery independently of its results, save when the slave had either forfeited his rights or had voluntarily surrendered them.

I have argued that a natural rights theory is likely to agree with utilitarianism that the property rights we have under elaborated modern systems are essentially conventional and artificial, and have to be justified by their role in aiding the recognition and enforcement of natural rights. To the extent that utilitarian elements enter into deciding what natural rights we have, there will be a considerable overlap in the kinds of property legitimated by the two moral perspectives. I hope that this also suggests what remains of natural rights theories when we abandon the attempt to derive them from the dictates of God, Nature and Reason. Whether by appeal to intuitive ideas about justice or by some other route, rights theorists seek to persuade us that a morality which reduces to instrumental considerations is inadequate.[22] We must recognize each individual as entitled to 'equal concern and respect', and that that entitlement 'trumps' other considerations. Given that such a claim is scarcely more precise in its implications for conduct than the utilitarian claim that happiness is the goal of all action and more of it better than less, we should expect a modern rights theory to be cautious in deriving any particular property regime from the bare idea that we have rights which either individuals nor the state may infringe.[23]

To this claim, there is one exception. This is where the conception of natural rights at stake is a proprietary one. The best, in all senses, exemplar of such a way of thinking is provided in Robert Nozick's *Anarchy, State and Utopia*. There, the basic thought is that we are born 'owning ourselves'. Where Locke had said that men have 'a property in' their own persons, Nozick's theory speaks of us as 'holdings'. Each of us possesses a freehold in ourselves. By the same token, none of us has any but negative rights against others, unless those others have conferred them upon us. As to what rights others may give us, their freehold in themselves implies that they may agree to absolutely anything. That this is a 'libertarian' theory of rights is evident. It follows instantly that 'victimless crimes' are a contradiction in terms; since it is *my* body, I may put what I like into it, and let others do to it anything I wish them to do and they are willing to do. Where Locke held that the law of nature forbade suicide it must follow from Nozick's view that suicide is no more to be forbidden than throwing out an old shirt. 'Whose life is it?' is the proper response to all 'moral legislation'.[24]

It is this view which launches the idea that all ownership is naturally ownership of an outright freehold. The world divides into objects which are owned and objects which are as yet unowned; all persons are self-owned — though if we were to wish to sell ourselves into slavery, it seems that there is nothing to prevent us doing so. If I have an idea, it is certainly not anyone else's; in having it I make it self-evidently 'mine', and I may do with it whatever I can (without infringing your proprietorship of whatever you are proprietor of). If I invent a new drug, I have no duty to provide it to the needy; I may sell it for whatever I can get — what I may not do is hamper anyone else who is legitimately trying to invent the same sort of drug or who can obtain it elsewhere on better terms. Whatever object as yet unowned by others falls into my hands without limiting the freedom of others to acquire whatever they may legitimately acquire is mine in freehold.[25]

Naturally, this argument goes terribly wrong when applied to any goods whose supply cannot be expanded indefinitely, the paradigm case of which is land; if more people wish to own land than there is land to go round, the first occupier's ownership does curtail the liberty of others and is therefore ruled out. Having seen this, Herbert Spencer in his radical youth called for the abolition of the landlord; Robert Nozick follows the later thoughts of Herbert Spencer in arguing that private ownership of land is so self-evidently all right that we must say (as Locke did) that the acquisition of unowned things is legitimate so long as it does not render others *worse off* than they would otherwise have been. As Nozick sees, this raises the question, 'worse off in what way?' and to this there is no simple answer. Locke faced fewer difficulties than Nozick, since he thought God had set the standards of the good life for man and had thus settled what it meant to say that private ownership of land was justified so long as 'a good living' was as available as before. God intended us to be able to secure 'a living' rather than a freehold. Nozick's universe has lost its Creator; if, therefore, we complain that our freedom to acquire land has been taken away, there is no way of telling us that we have not really had our freedom curtailed. To retort that we are all very much better off than we would have been had there been no private landed property will not do for this sort of natural rights theory. It would do for the utilitarian, but it will not do for the natural rights theorist who has to face the objection that he is justifying the violation of *my right* to appropriate land by appealing to the general (or even my) well-being. The point of thinking in proprietary terms is to avoid utilitarian considerations, not to succumb to them.[26]

Personality and Property

Given that theories of natural right pay sufficient attention to the individual's rights, but on a disputable foundation, while utilitarian theories square with a commonsense concern for the general welfare but not with individual rights, it is natural to look for some third way. One such was popular with the Idealists at the turn of the century, but can be detached from the Hegelian framework in which they worked, as it often has been since. The idea underlying their account of property, whether private or public, is that the foundation of morality is personality; the individual must be a member of a moral community which both recognizes the sanctity of the individual and sustains a view of the good life which will give meaning to the individual's existence. What mankind values is not merely happiness but the happiness which comes from a consciousness of having done one's duty, and having been rewarded according to one's merits.[1] As many writers have observed, it is not unhappiness which maddens us but injustice; by the same token, it is not mere pleasure which gratifies us but what one might call 'deserved well-being'.

This perspective is instrumental but not in a simple or 'maximizing' way. It is not utilitarian, therefore. It does not, however, see individual rights as 'trumps'; we have rights as members of a community, and our rights cannot 'trump' the highest good of that community. It follows that property rights must be assessed by way of their contribution to a society in which personality is most adequately expressed. Durkheim, who thought a conception of this kind was embedded in modern consciousness and ought therefore to be expressed in contemporary institutions, insisted that a merely utilitarian conception of individual property could not account for the outrage we feel at their violation; something close to 'sanctity' clings about them. He, like others attached to this mode of thought, did not think that this fact yielded any very simple account of what mixture of individual ownership and social control was proper; it does, however, yield a particular way of tackling the issue.[2]

At one extreme, it might be claimed that since personality is essentially embodied in single individuals, private property alone has any moral standing. Socialism is inconsistent with a proper respect for personality. At the other, it might be claimed that a society has a personality which can be expressed in socially owned property. Certainly, social ownership would have to be far more than merely a matter of handing privately owned firms or other property to a state appointed management. Quite what more is hard to say, but it would certainly involve institutional devices by means of which the requirements of society rather than the maximization of profit would be set up as the goal of the enterprise, and by which answerability to the workers within it would be part of the processes of management. It almost certainly would not be state socialism in the familiar Eastern European sense, because the state as the coercive arm of society would not embody enough of the collective personality of society as a whole.[3]

Whether this leads towards guild socialism or towards some mixture of private ownership and corporatist control, is a matter of local argument. The central thought is that individuals need both a space for free movement and secure social attachments, and that the institutions centred on the system of property rights must reflect that need. Rights reflect social functions, and individuals cannot, so to speak, stand on their rights against the social functions they fulfil. The secular analogue to Locke's claim that God made nothing for man to destroy is the thought that the function of property is to secure a morally worthwhile life for all members of society, so nobody can take refuge in the bare assertion that 'it's mine, so I will do what I like with it'.

On the issues we have suggested as the touchstones in assessing different justificatory theories, this 'personalist' approach yields some predictable answers. Slavery is evidently ruled out as firmly as under any theory of natural right, and more firmly than under a theory of natural right which gives us transferable freeholds in ourselves. One might, however, wonder whether personalist theories are quite invulnerable to the utilitarian suggestion that the violation of personality at various points in the past was necessary step towards a society in which personality is now recognized as inviolable. Kant denied that this kind of instrumental reasoning was legitimate; Hegel remarked obscurely that slavery belonged to a stage when wrong was right and temporarily valid.[4] The English Idealists followed Kant rather than Hegel. Many philosophers would hold that personalist theories of this kind try to balance on a vanishingly narrow knife-edge: if they retain an instrumental conception of rights, they cannot defend the thought that property in people is simply wrong, because it may sometimes be instrumentally essential in realizing the eventual triumph of personality; if they insist on the inviolability of the individual's rights, they then run into the problems faced by all natural rights theories, that of explaining how the inviolability arises and defending it against instrumentally powerful counter-examples. (May I really not take your bicycle against your will in order to deliver medicine to a dangerously ill person? If I may breach that property right, why not others? If others, why not in extremis even make a slave of someone?)

If slavery is handled (in spite of these doubts) more persuasively than by utilitarianism or pure natural rights theories, personalist justifications can be interesting, if indistinct, in their implications for landed property. Essentially, the argument is that if there is anything special about land it is less that it is finite and therefore scarce than that it is fixed.[5] This is, in its way, the moral theorist's version of the political theorist's old obsessions with stability. Landed property is capable of bearing the imprint of our activities — as all gardeners will attest; no doubt the depressed and put upon farm labourer sees in much of it no more than the record of back-breaking toil and mean living conditions, but even he may cherish the ploughed field as the record of a day well spent.

The ownership of land, therefore, offers opportunities for self-expression and allegiance, not simply for marketing farm produce or the extraction of urban rents by the slum landlord. What does this entail for the ownership of land? It is no simpler to answer that question than to answer the analogous question about public as opposed to private ownership. None the less, we may venture some answers. There is a prima facie case against the agricultural landlord-tenant relationship. The tenant improves the land, puts it into good heart, but gains no permanent relationship with it. Both in terms of the failure to provide an incentive to the tenant to cherish the land, and in terms of the injustice of severing the connection between effort and reward, old-fashioned rack renting comes off badly.[6] The personalist view of the matter absorbs these points into the personalist framework; what we want to achieve is a society in which individuals are so to speak anchored by their moral attachments and the rewards of doing their duty. An added evil of a relationship which is inefficient and unjust is that it must also fail to achieve that goal. Whether we try to create many smallholdings, or try by legislation to give tenants greater security and a financial interest in whatever they put into the land they use is a matter of prudence and local circumstances. But we shall not flinch from adjusting the relationship; the cry that landlords and tenants have come to an agreement which the law ought not to disturb is an appeal to the sanctity of contracts which is out of place in this context.

Lest this seem to slide too swiftly over difficulties in the personalist case, let me point out some of them. The largest of them is the objection that the personalist case is not a distinctive position, but is parasitic on other positions. The emphasis on individual character and fulfilment as a moral agent merely hides the extent to which ideals of justice or utilitarian considerations of welfare and economic growth do the real argumentative work, leaving 'personalism' to observe that if these other considerations are met the demands of morality are satisfied and moral agents who wish to see them satisfied will be gratified by the fact. This is a large objection; if it is sustained, but we do not feel entirely at ease with either a simple utilitarian calculus or a rigid insistence on natural right, we have nowhere much to go except for a commonsensical balancing of utilitarian and rights-based considerations. Even if it cannot be sustained, it may emerge that the personalist perspective still ends up performing such a balancing act, if not in a merely commonsensical way.[7]

The personalist response to the accusation that all an

emphasis on the satisfactions of distinctively moral agents is doing is taking in other theories' washing is to retort that in so doing it offers a perspective and a correction that other theories need not cannot provide. Utilitarians agree that what makes mankind happy at one time and place may not do so at another, but have nothing to say about which sorts of happiness and which times and places to prefer. An emphasis on the moral agent can distinguish between happiness worth having and happiness not worth having. Equally, an insistence on rights as trumps cannot by itself distinguish between justified self-defence and mere dog-in-the-manger resistance to legitimate demands from other people. An adequate theory of personality would do so.

Of course, if that reply is to convince, much more needs to be done to make it convincing. This is not the place to do it, but even this bare sketch may explain why the arguments I have christened 'personalist' have appealed to so many writers dissatisfied with the contractarian and natural rights based political theory of recent years. The personalist perspective is at home with the concerns of so-called 'communitarian' moral and political theories, since personality needs the right communal support if it is to flourish and communities are only worthy of our allegiance if they promote that personal flourishing. If such arguments do indeed leave us balancing rights-based and utilitarian considerations, they provide us with a context of argument in which to draw up the balance. We are not left with a flat conflict between, say, the demands of the general welfare and the existing property rights of the individual, rather, we can ask whether a community could flourish if it made these demands rather than those, whether the obdurate individual would on reflection find his or her loyalty stretched if existing expectations were not met.[8]

If this can be said for the perspective in general, we may still complain that its emphases are exaggerated. It blurs the reality of conflicts of interest, which is why it is less persuasive than simpler theories of rights, and why it is less persuasive than utilitarian theories which emphasize the possible gains to overall welfare from sacrificing one individual's welfare to that of the rest. By suggesting that the individual and the community flourish together or not at all they hide the reality which demands moral reflection in the first place. Or, we may wonder whether it exaggerates the extent to which we require a community to reflect back to us the moral aspirations it inculcates in us. One might, for instance, agree with thinkers of a personalist persuasion that capitalism in its purest and most uninhibited form is essentially arbitrary, casino-like and nothing but a controlled version of Hobbes's 'war of all against all' — but go on to defend it.[9] If the casino economy produces the goods, we may suppose that the rest of social life, the family, religious institutions, cultural life generally will provide an adequate outlet for expressive and altruistic aspirations. We know that people slip easily and painlessly from one role to another; they are capable of spending their working days in the war of all against all, while remaining loving parents and spouses, devoted churchgoers, contributors to charity, energetic public spirited citizens and so on. In that case, no particular conclusions about property rights can be drawn from considerations of personality.

The personalist reply is tentative rather than conclusive. In part, it must be negative, in that it depends on denying that people are quite as flexible and deft at role-switching as the sceptic suggests; some are, but not all. Those who are will naturally thrive under casino conditions and will support the system which enables them to flourish; those who do not thrive will almost certainly be less articulate. That fact suggests that even the free wheeling casino operator preserves his own moral confidence only because he lives in a community which reflects and reinforces his individual aspirations, and this opens the way to more positive arguments. If the casino suits some people, it may suit fewer than it alienates. The personalist wishes as many people as possible to experience what he or she regards as a satisfying life, and therefore wishes either to insulate the self-interested world of the capitalist economy from other social institutions or else to go further in controlling the acquisition and disposal of property.[10]

This may not always be a movement in a distinctively socialist direction, if we think of socialism as a mixture of public ownership, egalitarianism in the distribution of welfare, and radical democracy in politics. It might be a movement of a conservative sort.[11] Indeed, this is so obviously true that socialist movements have had to go to extraordinary lengths to prevent their members from succumbing to conservative offers of protection from the rigours of unbridled capitalism, at the price of hierarchy and paternalism. Not everyone believes passionately in the importance of political equality and political participation; anyone who does not do so will think it equally likely that a conservative control over the operations of the marketplace and what people may do with their property will achieve what the personalist regards as the good life as that socialism will. To get further than this stand-off further premises are needed.

Property and Liberty

We have already tackled the connection between property and
the classical conception of political liberty; I shall end this
book with a consideration of the distinctively Marxian perspective on property, alienation and freedom. Here, we must
briefly examine three ways in which moral justifications and
criticisms of ownership rights connect with freedom. The first
way is in their response to the thought that acquisition and
ownership limit the freedom of non-owners and therefore
pose a moral problem; the second is the attempt to derive
ownership directly from the thought that individuals are free
agents whose freedom is not to be overridden save to protect
the freedom of others.[1] We shall not spend very long on that
argument, for it will turn out to be the 'proprietary' interpretation of natural rights theory under a different label.
Lastly, we must examine the argument that property rights can
create freedom, enhance individual autonomy, and liberate us
from natural and social constraints of various kinds. This has
something in common with utilitarian arguments for ownership rights, but only something; it has more in common with
Hume's enthusiasm for the 'brisk march of the spirits'.[2] It can
also supply the basis for a modern defence of property as an
aid to pluralism and the dispersion of power, and therefore to
political liberty. I hope that by the end of this chapter, therefore, something of a unification of the concerns of the first
two parts of this book will have been achieved.

The proposition that the acquisition of property limits the
freedom of non-owners is self-evidently true, if we think that
property in anything means *inter alia* that other persons are
not at liberty to use, consume, alter or otherwise deal with
whatever it is without the owner's leave.[3] It is however hard to
visualize the way property, and rights more generally, limit
the liberty of others. Although property rights confer de jure

control, over ourselves we always have de facto control, so it is difficult to think oneself into a context in which one can contemplate the ideas and abilities of individuals as also part of the unowned 'stuff' of the world. The priority of our own de facto ability to control what we do over anyone else's right to achieve the same result demands an extraordinary leap of the imagination from anyone trying to visualize an entirely 'ownerless' world. John Rawls's *Theory of Justice* requires such an effort of the imagination, when he asks us to contemplate a world before we have invented justice in which everything is part of the common pool of resources over which nobody in particular has any rights.[4]

Once we have made that leap of imagination, it is evident that my exercise of de jure or de facto control over my abilities limits your freedom to use them as you choose, and similarly for your abilities and my freedom. The question then becomes that of what justifies the limitation of each person's freedom involved in the existence of other people's property rights. This was the way Henry Sidgwick framed the question in his *Elements of Politics*. Its answer for Sidgwick had to take a utilitarian turn. My free access to whatever I sought to use was limited by arrangements which paid off in benefits which I could not have had but for the institution of property.[5]

That this rules out the 'ownership' of persons by anyone other than themselves is not hard to see; since we are visualizing a situation in which we are seeking each person's assent to the curtailing of his or her liberty, we are forced to show that it is a good bargain to each of them. We cannot show this to the slave, who emerges as having no stake in the system. We could reach a similar if weaker conclusion by demonstrating that the de facto control which even the slave exercises over his own body — slavery works on the body by working on the will — means that a system of free labour will be more productive and more progressive than any other, and that the limits on the free access to the activities and abilities of others which that imposes on each of us therefore pay off in added welfare.

But, what this argument does not do is show when *freedom* as distinct from welfare will be maximized. What we are after now, however, is an argument to show that the limitation of freedom imposed by the recognition of property rights is a step to the maximization of freedom. Many writers have doubted whether any such argument can be produced.[6] While it may be possible under some conditions to say that there has been an increase or decrease in general freedom, there can be no precise argument over how much increase or decrease there has been, let alone an argument about what arrangements will maximize liberty. Some have gone further. Even in the kind of case where we incline to think freedom has been increased, we are wrong; suppose we disarm a gunman, thus allowing a dozen people previously coerced by him to escape that coercion — the temptation is to say that a dozen are now free, while at the worst one is no longer free to to coerce them. I incline to say this, but it has been argued that what has been altered is only the distribution of liberty; formerly, all control belonged to the man with the gun, now to all of them separately.

There is no very obvious way of resolving all the issues this view raises. The simplest retort is to point out that freedom is not only a question of control, but primarily one of a particular sort of control, namely coercion. Removing the gunman frees the whole dozen because it removes the source of coercion. If this is plausible, we may make the first step to showing that private property in some form or other maximizes freedom by arguing that it reduces to a minimum the extent to which the use of goods and abilities is coercively dictated. Certainly, the law's coercive capacity makes it possible for us to enjoy the de jure ownership the law grants us; but we may doubt whether any other arrangement would be as economical of coercion.[7] A 'free for all' would be 'coercive for all' as the strong battled it out with each other or with leagues of the weak.[8] Moreover, the utilitarian considerations earlier adduced might be expected to play a role in diminishing even the coercive character of the law. The thought that the law says 'touch this person's goods or capacities without his or her permission at your peril' is not the only thought we may entertain. We may equally see the law representing a consensus that 'according to ways of coordinating our production and consumption favoured round here, this person is uniquely entitled to say how these goods and capacities should be used'. Particular distributions of property rights would not be coercively arrived at and one might justly think that a person who is

liable to coercion only when he or she fails to keep a freely
arrived at bargain is hardly coerced at all. 'If I fail to keep my
word, you may make me do so' is a long way from being the
victim of simple brute force.

This view is entirely consistent with Hume's insistence that
as a matter of history most legal systems originated in force
and fraud. That the first owners of things were those who
seized them, hung on to them, and finally got everyone else to
accept the legitimacy of 'first possession' may or may not be
true. To the present generation, origins are irrelevant. The
question is whether settled property rights with associated
legal security for contract, inheritance and other elaborations
of ownership rights minimize the coercive element in production and distribution.[9] The answer is doubtless that it all
depends. If the owners of property are able to do as the first
generation of American capitalist barons did and buy up legislatures, police forces, judges and anything else they needed to
get their own way, it is highly implausible to think that this is
the state of minimal coercion. But, this does not impugn the
thought that a secure system of property rights *would* be minimally coercive; the hoodlums employed by Gould, Rockefeller
and the like were engaging in extra-legal coercion to secure what
they could not secure if everyone's property rights were
respected — such as cheap way leaves for railways and pipe-
lines without which their fortunes would not have been made.[10]

It is to be noted that if 'non-coercion' is the dimension of
freedom we are concerned with, attacks on the idea that a
secure system of individual property could be minimally *coercive* are sociological rather than philosophical. That is, they
rest on the thought, either that the existing system of rights
originated in force and fraud and still betrays the marks of its
birth, or that private property breeds inequalities of wealth
which spill over into inequalities of power. Thus, Marx's
denunciation of capitalist exploitation relies in part on the fact
that capitalism originated in the forcible expropriation of
small farmers; they were thrown off the land, and offered the
non-choice of working as labourers or starving. Since they
were thus held to ransom, their wage contracts were not freely
made; their low wages and their employers' profits were both
to be explained as a form of robbery, disguised by the contractual appearances.[11] Marx's other attacks on exploitation

rest on the thought that workers contribute more to the product than they receive, while capitalists contribute nothing and take the profits, but this has nothing to do with coercion, save to the extent that unequal access to resources has to be explained by the historical argument above.

Some philosophers have tried to make more of the fact that behind property rights there stands the coercive power of the law. However, in making more of it, they have perfectly properly moved away from the narrow notion of freedom as non-coercion to the wider notion of freedom as 'non-prevention' — the law's coercive power is what prevents you treating my bicycle as an object in the public domain, but my simple refusal to till your field might prevent you using my efforts, regardless of property rights.[12] It is not that in owning my own efforts, I have a coercive power over you which prevents you from using my efforts, but that my bare physical ability to resist is enough to stop you. So we have to ask whether any particular system of property rights can be defended as minimizing the degree to which we are prevented or obstructed in fulfilling our goals.

The difficulty with this question is our lack of a metric for obstructedness or preventedness. The obvious route is to suggest that we are more prevented when that we are prevented from doing or having access to is more important to us. So, if you will starve unless I till the field, my ability to say no is a great obstacle; if you do not need what I would produce, it is hardly an obstacle at all. This, however, runs into two problems; the first is that importance collapses rather easily into utilitarian considerations again. It is not the extent of your loss of freedom which is determined by the extent of your need for my efforts but the extent to which your welfare would be increased if I cooperated. Unless 'obstructedness' is to mean more than 'unable to have as much as would do us good' there is no point in taking this route. The second problem is that preventedness is better measured by the degree of difficulty in evading the obstacle than by the amount of good its evasion would do me. This is why the defenders of private ownership are unabashed by most of the arguments of their critics. The free market with a multiplicity of independent buyers and sellers minimizes the difficulty of evading the obstructions placed in one's way by one recalcitrant owner of goods or abilities. One nationalized industry is less avoidable than a multitude of competing smaller enterprises; monopoly is the enemy of freedom thus construed.[13]

Wisely, Marx shifted the argument onto somewhat different ground, arguing that what each proletarian faced was the capitalist class. Each capitalist was forced by the logic of the situation to behave just like every other capitalist, and the proletarian could only avoid one capitalist's terms for allowing him to live by accepting the same terms from another. Conversely, he sometimes wrote as if the proletariat as a class was the proper object of moral interest; that any single proletarian might evade the constraints of his position was irrelevant when set beside the fact that one could climb out of the proletariat only if the others did not. The class had to be emancipated as a class.[14]

By this stage in the argument, we have moved a long way from the minimization of coercion in its everyday sense. It may well be true that being propertiless in a capitalist society severely limits the options available to you; it may also be true that we jointly exercise less control over our fates under a system of private ownership and the free market than we might under a yet to be realized — or adequately described — system of common ownership. These issues must wait until we have dealt with the second strand of arguments connecting property and liberty.

This, simply, maintains that property is an outgrowth of liberty. Individuals' 'property in' themselves is displayed in their control of their own behaviour and their dislike of interference. It is not their right to engage in this behaviour and display this resistance which has to be defended but any suggestion that they do not have such rights: I may put my foot where I like, but not on top of your hand. If there is nothing to defeat the right to act freely (as there is in that instance), then we have the right. The possession of such a right is not backed by coercion and can be described independently of any notion of coercion. To have a right is simply to have a liberty which others ought to recognize. Under what conditions we may coerce others into recognizing it is another question; whether other people have a duty to assist us in defending it is another question still.[15]

This view connects liberty and property by arguing that so

long as individuals use only what is theirs, they cannot limit the liberty of others. Liberty is maximized, indeed 'natural liberty' is unscathed, if everyone employs only what is theirs to employ and refrains from employing what is not theirs. The only way liberty is invaded is by incursions on what is not ours. We have here the classical defence of the 'simple system of natural liberty' beloved of Adam Smith.[16]

It should be noticed, however, that this vision rests on what it wishes to conclude. It is a restatement of the proprietary account of natural right, given a libertarian gloss. Unlike the first attempt to derive property from freedom, which began from the Hobbesian starting point that in the absence of enforceable rules we are free to do anything, even as Hobbes said, 'to use one another's bodies', this starts from the thought that the rights of others do not limit our freedom. We cannot be free to violate other people's rights; rights so to speak set the frame-work within which discussions of freedom can take place.[17]

Those who were persuaded of the merits of this theory before will need no further persuasion. Those who were not will see that once again we are faced with the argument that if we care for non-interference with individual action we must allow individuals to acquire freeholds in external goods. The question again reduces to the question whether conceding an individual the right to act as he chooses, and do what he chooses so long as he does not infringe the like liberty in others, also concedes the power to acquire freehold ownership. The right to act freely so long as we do not infringe the like right in others plainly comes closer to founding ownership than does the right to act harmlessly. The range of justifications for stopping anyone taking and using what he wishes and engaging in bargains with others for the use of what they have taken is more limited. Whereas it is plain that competition from someone else harms me, and may therefore be a ground for complaint (doubtless to be overridden by the public interest in cheapness and good service in nine cases out of ten) it is less clear that competition restricts my liberty.

This is not to say that conventional freeholds are easily derived from the right to free action. They require a good deal more social support than mere non-interference, which most free action does not. Anything resembling a will, for instance,

requires the positive cooperation of others; my current desires
for what happens after my death may provide a reason for
others to help me to realize them, but I need their help after my
death, not their mere non-interference before it. Nor is it only
posthumous events for which I need help; I should be equally
unable to impose restrictive covenants on anything I formerly
used and possessed unless others assisted in their enforcement.
In general, just as 'harmless use' will only generate rights
themselves bounded by their defensibility as instances of
harmless use, so the right to undisturbed possession and use
would always derive from what the first acquisition derived
from, namely the fact that what I acquired, I could acquire
and use without limiting the like liberty of others. My present
right does not rest on a natural property right. In general,
any argument which rests so heavily on the right to act in
any way that does not infringe the like liberty of others
must rely only on such considerations; it cannot change tack
to rely on 'it's mine' as the basis of a claim to assistance. It
is true that to many people the distinction between a gift inter
vivos and a bequest after death appears to be slight; none the
less, it is enough to show that property is the gift of convention rather than nature, however natural the convention might
seem.[18]

This implies that we may retain a concern for freedom and a
concern for rights without being committed thereby to the
acceptance of an untrammelled system of private ownership
and the free market. We must therefore turn to the third route
from freedom to ownership. We have been steering towards
the thought that freedom is several-layered; it involves the
absence of coercion, and it involves the absence of other, less
definite obstacles which human beings may place in the way of
other people achieving their goals. On most people's view of
freedom, however, it also involves the expansion of our
options. This is a difficult point to make with any precision;
we must not collapse freedom into ability, for it is clear that
'free to leave, but unable to do so' and similar descriptions
are not contradictions in terms. Yet it is counter-intuitive to
suggest that increased abilities do nothing to enlarge our
liberty. 'Freedom of choice' implies a wide range of options;
Helvetius's claim that it is no loss of liberty not to be able to
soar like the eagle or swim like the whale does not quite seem to

deny that it would enlarge our options if we could do either or both of those things.[19]

At all events, one of the more persuasive routes from freedom to ownership is to point to the increased options which the invention of ownership brings about. Without guarantees of future control over the objects of ownership, we cannot create novel objects, cannot engage in exploratory economic and productive behaviour. Property allows us to contract with one another for future performance conditional on half-predictable events taking place — *if* I manage to sail right round the world and come back with a vessel full of gold and spices, *then* I will pay you half of the proceeds. Who would sail round the world otherwise — or, more crucially, who would finance the voyage? Innovation, imagination, creativity are the terms to conjure with. This is not a utilitarian argument, because it cares too little for being able to assess our success in satisfying pre-existing desires. It is a libertarian argument, because it cares about our being able to expand our options.[20]

Like any such argument, it may or may not pay particular attention to each individual singly, as opposed to the whole species. The old instrumental argument for slavery may or may not shelter here; if property rights are to increase everyone's options and nobody is to be a mere means to an end, slavery falls at the first fence — as it must in, say, John Rawls's understanding of such arguments. If it is the human species whose options are to increase, the slave may, unfairly no doubt, be one of the victims of a process which is justified on the whole — as it is in Hegel, Marx or Mill writing in this vein. How we, now, should feel about the 'caryatids supporting the dancing floor of the future' is an unresolved question; Hegel robustly refused to wince, Marx denounced all pre-socialist societies as pre-human, and Mill winced while insisting that the balance of advantage lay with sacrificing the primitive few to the developed many.[21] Without the Athenian slave, no modern Europe; without modern Europe, no liberty.

It is this argument for freedom, characterized often enough as 'progress', which one finds in Hayek's defence of private property and the free market. He is quite clear that it is not a utilitarian argument, because the glory of the system is that we find out what we want and what it is possible to have; we do not adjust known means to predefined ends. Were we of fixed natures, utilitarianism would lead to a planned society; we should know how to optimize the use of all available resources, and the argument for an unplanned society would have gone. It is precisely the openness of human nature and the indeterminacy of what is available to satisfy our desires which justifies an emphasis on private ownership. Freedom is in many ways a better justification of the process than progress; progress suggests that there is some unequivocal standard against which progress can be measured, while an argument of this sort strongly suggests that there is not. The best we can do is to say that when offered more freedom of choice, people generally but not always take it. We may feel less contented than our forbears but we do not wish to go back to the society they inhabited.

Does option enlargement unequivocally favour private property as usually understood? It is doubtful that it does.[22] It must favour whatever encourages entrepreneurial vision and energy; but it is not clear that private property and free markets are the *only* recipe for what we want. Suppose we find that an economy so based favours monetary rewards over non-monetary ones and therefore limits the possibilities; suppose we find that such an economy tends to prefer the very short run to the medium and long run, and is therefore not very innovative after all, because it does not devote enough resources to research and development. Can we not interfere with the choices owners make in order to promote option enlargement at a certain cost in coercive intervention? The objections to so doing would have to be technical rather than principled — the fear that once intervention began it could never be stopped, or that it would create so many secondary disturbances that innovation would slow down after all. We might also fear that intervention would be costly in other ways. Setting up firms which offered workers a different set of choices between income yielding work and leisure from that offered in the market place might mean setting up firms which made such vast losses that the exercise was pointless. None the less, these are at most technical possibilities. The only argument which rules out intervention in principle is the natural rights argument we saw little reason to accept.[23]

If a concern to minimize coercive measures for the organization of production and distribution means that we generally prefer markets to bureaucracies, and a concern for option enlargement means that we adopt whatever eclectic strategies we think will work to produce liveliness and innovation, the last plank in the theory must be the connection between property rights and the preservation of social and political liberty. Here we are finishing the unfinished business of Part One. There we ended inconclusively, suggesting that the old questions of how to secure stability, loyalty and constitutionality were live issues still, but that an effort of the imagination was required to see how to translate the property-based prescriptions of earlier centuries into plausible contemporary terms.

One possibility is to change direction somewhat and take up the thought that 'only power can check power'; then the liberal defence of private property comes to saying that the dispersion of property disperses power.[24] Suppose we consider the ability of individuals to protest against some government measure. Unless they can collect the resources to publicize their dissent, they are hampered; unless they can secure transport to their meetings, they are hampered; unless they are sure that their protests will not jeopardize their livelihood they are hampered. Will private property help? It is obviously not a sufficient condition. The South African press is privately owned but fiercely censored; on the other hand, it is infinitely more outspoken than the Soviet press. Nobody doubts that what deters the South African regime from yet more ferocious incursions into press freedom is less the ability of the press to cause it trouble locally than the need to preserve some sort of relationship with western powers.

Similarly, the press and almost all of industry was privately owned under the Nazis, but the regime's capacity for straightforward brutality and its enthusiastic readiness to resort to it wiped out any assistance that that might have offered to the would-be dissenter. If private property is an aid to political liberty, it can only be in conjunction with much else, such as a tradition of dissent which encourages individuals to employ their resources and discourages governments from putting the balance of power to the test. Prewar Fascism and Nazism suggest that a liberal tradition is more to the point than private property.[25]

This, however, is not to deny that it may well be easier to preserve political liberty if we can preserve a degree of social and intellectual liveliness, and that it may well be easier to preserve that if we encourage the dispersion of private property. This goal itself may well require positive measures to reduce tendencies to monopoly and cartelization. Quite what combination of open opportunity, resource dispersion and social training gives us the best chance of such social liveliness is very hard to say. It is plain that many societies have had a great dispersion of property and a passionate attachment to private ownership — peasant France and Eire for instance — with no social liveliness and no taste for intellectual, social and moral innovation, nor in the case of France with much taste for democracy and political liberalism either. Once again, we find ourselves driven to the conclusion that *if* people have the right temperament and ambitions, *then* possession of the appropriate resources will be a great help. The resources will hardly do the trick on their own.

Those who would like decisive conclusions for private or public ownership will not be happy to have reached so indecisive a stopping place. All the same, anything more uninhibited would be an exercise in bad faith. The historical record is that only those modern societies with some kind of a capitalist economy based on private property and the market have been innovative, politically liberal and intellectually progressive. But there have been enough examples of tyranny combined with a capitalist economy to induce caution.[26] Moreover, the most successful societies on all these fronts have been those which have managed either a 'social market economy' or some semi-socialist compromise. My own view is that the most interesting moral arguments for one's preferred forms of ownership are those based on freedom; they pick up what is attractive in 'personalist' theories, move directly to what makes natural rights theories attractive without incurring the metaphysical anxieties those theories induce in most of us, and have a vision of human well-being which is not tied to the implausibilities of classical utilitarianism. But anybody who doubts that may still accompany me a good deal of the way so long as he or she accepts that the moral theories I have sketched here have to take in a lot of each other's washing. That none of them can make the world less complicated than it happens in fact to be is not a defect in them, whether or not it is a defect in the world.

PART THREE:

THE LIFE AND DEATH

OF PROPERTY RIGHTS

The third focus of interest in property rights is historical. The history of views about the history of property rights is a subject of some interest. Because the law of property is so much a question of the pedigree of claimed and disputed rights, law has had a strongly historical character in every society with a developed legal system.[1] Deriving present claims from past practices almost compels a reflective lawyer to consider how rights have changed and with them the wider assumptions which give them life. For all that, the law in day to day operation takes an interest in the past only for the sake of justifying or rebutting the claims put forward by individuals and institutions in the present. It is legal, economic or social historians who have taken the greatest interest in the virtues and vices of property institutions more generally. Most histories have been justificatory and present-centred; others have been equally present-centred but condemnatory. Others — though fewer — have tried to escape the political struggle and gratify a legitimate curiosity about the development of a major social institution. This section discusses the view of the history of property associated with the 'economic theory of law' and ends with the Marxian vision of the role of property in the history of alienated man and the claim that liberation will be accomplished in a propertyless world. It begins, however, with the pre-history of both these perspectives, with the Enlightenment visions of Rousseau and the Scottish historians of the later eighteenth century.

Liberation and Slavery

Lurking in much of the 'political' debate over property is an implicit theory of history. Without recapitulating most of what was discussed in Part One, we may take up the story in the eighteenth-century, partly because that was when the social history of institutions in its modern guise was developed in Scotland by such men as John Millar, John Robertson and Adam Ferguson, and partly because that was when the idea of 'modernity' seized hold of the historical imagination.[2] Even if Harringtonian 'ancient prudence' was looked to for a model of social understanding, it was firmly understood by the modernizers that nothing could bring back the world of the ancient city state. Ferguson and Rousseau regretted the virtues of 'rude societies' in a way that Hume and Smith did not. Neither thought those virtues could be reintroduced to modern society.

This detachment from their own allegiances was a factor in their writing a sociologially serious history of institutions. The Scots writers in particular linked the general progress of society from a 'rude' to a 'polite' condition to property, to class differentiation, and to the impact of these on forms of government — which in their turn promoted or resisted changes in legal forms and social relations. Even where this picked up the social and political concerns of earlier writers, it was a genuine intellectual novelty. Marx thought of the Scottish historians and Rousseau as precursors of his own materialist conception of history, and in outline, it is true that theirs was a recipe for writing an adequate social history which twentieth-century writers would be happy to accept.[3]

The commonly accepted framework saw human history as a

four stage process, beginning in primitive hunting and gathering and culminating — for the moment — in modern commercial society. The first stage of human existence must have been an exceedingly simple hand to mouth one. Men wandered the face of the earth in small groups or single families, catching game and picking the fruits of nature as best they could. A simple division of labour allowed men to hunt while women looked after children; and there must have been enough elementary cooperation to make hunting more effective rather than less. That cooperation would have demanded very simple 'quasi-property' rules. If only the man who actually killed the hunted animal got to eat it, beaters to drive the game onto the spears of the hunters would have been hard to recruit; some principled division of the spoils was required. These would not have amounted to explicit rules about property, because next to nothing would have outlasted the day, and the group which cooperated to catch its dinner would appropriate the catch as a group. 'In a tribe which subsists by hunting and fishing, the arms, the utensils and the fur which the individual carries are to him the only subjects of property. The food of to-morrow is yet wild in the forest or hid in the lake; it cannot be appropriated before it is caught; and even then, being the purchase of numbers, who fish or hunt in a body, it accrues to the community, and is applied to immediate use, or becomes an accession to the stores of the public.'[4]

Political authority would have been absent, because there would have been nothing for authority to do and no sanctions with which to enforce its word. The need not to fight or insult each other, not to snatch the food from each other's hands, and to avoid provoking sexual jealousy is so obvious that everyday morality enforces the rules which satisfy that need. In the terms of H.L.A. Hart's *Concept of Law*, 'primary' rules alone would have been recognized.[5] Though passion might inflame men to fight or abuse one another, there was no lasting benefit to be gained by doing so, and so no need for permanent laws or police. With no need for authority nor any surplus to pay those who exercised it, there was no authority. 'Where no profit attends dominion, one party is as much averse to the trouble of perpetual command, as the other is to the mortification of perpetual submission.'[6]

The 'four stage' view of history supposed that mankind

moved from hunting and gathering to pasturage, then to agriculture and finally to commerce. There was no unanimity
about the process by which mankind moved on from the original savage condition — though the universal view that this
was the aboriginal condition is a (small) part of the story of the
English unconcern for the customary rights of aboriginal
populations encountered during colonization. Writers who
thought human history reflected a more or less intrinsic
human rationality might appeal to the obvious advantages of
pastoral life compared with hunting and gathering and so
imply that the hunters and gatherers invented the next, or
pastoral stage; writers who were inclined to see humanity as
feckless until driven to thought were more likely to suggest
that population growth had pushed the need to domesticate
animals onto even simpler societies.[7] None suggested that
there was an inexorable necessity requiring a movement from
one stage to the next or forbidding society to 'skip' a stage: the
American Indians engaged in a little agriculture, but had never
been pastoralists. Nor were hunters and gatherers always con-
vinced of the need to move onto the next evolutionary rung.
As Ferguson observed, 'It was a proverbial imprecation in use
among the hunting nations on the confines of Siberia, that
their enemy might be obliged to live like a Tartar, and be seized
with the folly of breeding and attending his cattle. Nature, it
seems, in their apprehension, by storing the woods and the
deserts with game, rendered the task of the herdsman unneces-
sary, and left to man only the trouble of selecting and seizing
his prey.'[8] The American Indian, so often used as the clinching
argument, had few domestic animals and practised only the
most casual gardening, because there were endless herds of
bison to be hunted and no population pressures on the existing
mode of life.

As society developed through a mode of subsistence which
depended on tending their flocks to one which depended on
agriculture, so property rights became more definite and more
extensive. Pastoralists needed, and therefore had, much more
sophisticated property rights; who would tend and rear infant
sheep if they could not rely on enjoying the milk, wool and
other fruits of their husbandry?[9] Moreover, it was well worth
stealing a sheep where it had not been worth stealing fruit or
fish or game which could be legitimately obtained with no

more effort than it would take to steal them. So private property in animals and in the offspring of animals came into the world. Land, on the other hand, remained common; nobody needed, so nobody tried to enforce, rights which lasted longer than occupancy by one's flocks. Years before, Locke had employed against Filmer's attempt to link patriarchy and the divine right of kings the fact that Abraham was a pastoral clan chieftain, not a territorially based monarch. The characteristic political and legal form of all pastoral societies was the patriarchally governed tribe wandering the earth from one grazing ground to another.

The decisive step was not the introduction of agriculture alone (for, as we have seen, the American Indians had a version of that) but that of agriculture based on efficient techniques for making metal ploughshares and other implements. Rousseau's *Discourse on the Origins of Inequality* states the case in a way that struck Adam Smith and almost all its readers: 'The poets tell us it was gold and silver, but, for the philosophers, it was iron and corn which first civilized men and ruined humanity. Thus both were unknown to the savages of America who for that reason are still savage; the other nations also seem to have continued in a state of barbarism while they practised only one of these arts.'[10] Rousseau, who deplored the process, depicted it as one in which 'work became indispensable, and vast forests became smiling fields, which man had to water with the sweat of his brow, and where slavery and misery were soon seen to germinate and grow up with the crops.'[11] Mandeville had celebrated all such changes as steps towards the corrupt but lively state of civilization; for Rousseau, they were not steps to liberty but to slavery. Inequality riveted chains of dependence on the poor and chains of self-deception on their superiors. 'One man thinks himself the master of others and yet remains a greater slave than they.'[12] Adam Smith agreed that agricultural settlement and the creation of property in land was the prelude to inequality as well as the basis of the growth of law and settled political authority; but Smith also insisted that since productivity vastly increased, the rich were led by an invisible hand to provide the poor with at least as many of the real necessities of life as they could have secured under natural equality.[13] As to the delightful picture of the indolent life of the savage painted by Rousseau, Smith faced both ways; sometimes he suggested that the beggar sunning himself by the side of the road had as secure and agreeable an existence as the sovereign, but more generally insisted that industriousness, self-control and an end to ignorance were themselves progress and were among the valuable side-effects of the rise of property. Where Rousseau saw economic discipline as slavery, Smith was nearer to seeing it as liberation from the limitations of our primitive nature.[14]

The establishment of agriculture demanded the establishment of fixed property in land. Without it, tenure would have been precarious, the incentive to labour diminished and productivity damaged. Eighteenth-century writers had a clear sense of what was implied by the development of property. It meant that security of title took priority over everything else. Where simpler societies had been able to rely on rough and ready rules for the occasions when famine or whatever were agreed to allow the hungry to take what they needed from the supplies of the rich, economic development meant a sharper distinction between the legal rules which gave men legally recognized rights and duties and the moral rules which were unenforceable but which softened the hardships which strict legality could not.[15]

Smith lectured on jurisprudence as part of his duties at Glasgow and offered the conjectural history of the development of property that we have been following here. Whatever the scholarly purposes of the course, one major concern had been to show that civilization was, on the whole, a good bargain even to the poor. This tied in with his purely jurisprudential concerns when he tried to show how his theory of moral sentiments — based on the idea that morality rested on a kind of disinterested sympathy — could explain the standard Roman Law rules for gaining ownership and passing it on. Smith claimed that 'the impartial spectator' who resided in the bosom of every calm and conscientious person would accept the validity of the so-called natural modes of acquisition and would approve such familiar features of Roman and common law as the rule that delivery must take place before ownership could pass. The impartial spectator, generalizing from his own needs, would be moved by the usefulness of such legal provisions, not in a simple utilitarian way, but in a way which combined the utilitarian concern for the general welfare

with an 'impartial' concern that everyone should gain something from the law's protection of the propertied.[16]

This was both like and unlike the way Hume treated the
same issues. Hume — free of professorial duties as he was —
was less interested in the minutiae of the legal provisions of
Roman Law, more interested in pointing out the absurdities of
appealing to any sort of social contract in explaining the
origins of justice, property and government. Like Smith,
however, he took it for granted that property rights grew up in
response to the need for security of expectation — of the
goods which any of us enjoys, some, such as honour and
esteem, can be lost but cannot be stolen; external goods,
however, can be stolen. If I destroy your good name, I do not
improve my own; if I steal your cattle, I do increase my herd.
'Property' is taken by Hume to mean all rights over external
objects of value. It is this that leads him to say, what would
otherwise seem very odd, that justice and property arise
together.[17] Were men to be spontaneously altruistic, or goods
to be not at all scarce, property rights would have no point;
there would be no need for rules to assign priority to some
claims over others, and no need for authority to deter one man
from invading another's rights. If 'justice' is understood as
'suum cuique tribuere', Hume is quite right that in the absence
of rules of 'meum and tuum' there would be no justice.

Hume was no more inclined than Smith to suggest that a
rational appraisal of utility would go the whole way in explaining the actual development of institutions. Far from treating
institutions as deliberately designed to increase utility, Hume
relied on appeals to the 'imagination' to explain most of what
he thought worth explaining — which was just as we should
expect from a philosopher who had already explained causa-
tion and our belief in the existence of an external world in
terms of habit and imagination.[18] It was, for example, natural
to associate the offspring with the parent, and therefore
natural to adopt both the rule that the owner of a domestic
animal owned the animal's young, and the rule that the owner's children had first claim on their parents' property. Imagination was not a wholly fixed quality of the mind; it obeyed
the rules of the association of ideas, and what it came up
with would depend on circumstances. Hume held that utility
explained the existence of rules about property, but the

imagination explained the local details of such rules.

This aspect of the argument is an extension of the moral and political philosophy of Hume and Smith, almost more than a reflection of their historical concerns. Smith's calmest reflections on economic history belong to the *Wealth of Nations* rather than to his *Lectures on Jurisprudence*. It is in that multifaceted treatise that he faces the argument which Rousseau, Millar and Robertson also engaged with. The existence of settled property in land is the crucial stage in the origins of inequality. Until then, such inequalities as there were were personal and adventitious; the braver, the stronger, the better-looking no doubt enjoyed an ascendancy over others, and fared better than their fellows in love and in war; the old and wise secured a measure of personal respect for their wisdom. None of this offered a basis for class inequality. The arrival of fixed proprietorship in land did so. It is the permanent division of mankind into rich and poor, the propertied and the unpropertied, which Rousseau regarded as 'slavery'. Legal, or at any rate recognized forms of slavery are evidently possible in any condition where one man can keep another permanently under his control; pastoralists could abduct women or young men from neighbouring tribes and set them to work or to breed. But they might escape, and if not were likely to assimilate to their new society. What Rousseau detested was the inherited subordinate status which was the lot of the majority in all countries where economic inequality reigned.[19] Inequality of wealth, esteem and power were mutually implicated; wealth meant power and power meant wealth, the rich and powerful came to believe in their own superiority and frequently persuaded the poor to believe in it too. If property was the root of all evil, it led to particular political evils becaus property required a state to protect it.

Smith does not trouble to dispute Rousseau's picture of the way the state originated; it is the present rather than the past that Smith defends against him. Rousseau invites us to consider the effects, not just of property in land, but of cumulative inheritance and its effects on the competitive spirit. The rich man suffers vicarious anxiety in every item of his possessions and seeks a cure: 'Destitute of valid reasons to justify and sufficient strength to defend himself, able to crush individuals with ease, but easily crushed himself by a troop of

bandits, one against all, and incapable, on account of mutual
jealousy, of joining with his equals against numerous enemies
united by the common hope of plunder, the rich man, thus
urged by necessity, conceived at length the profoundest plan
that ever entered the mind of man: this was to employ the
forces of those who attacked him, to make allies of his adver-
saries, to inspire them with different maxims, and to give them
other institutions as favourable to himself as the law of nature
was unfavourable.'[20] Of course, the rich never say, 'protect
our advantages, and in return we will govern and exploit you'.
They offer the impartial protection of the law to everyone; but
since the law must by definition protect the haves against the
have-nots, the rich get a great deal more out of the bargain
than the poor.

Smith's response, as we have seen, was to observe that even
if the existence of law favoured the rich, it also favoured the
poor. This argument has become famous in recent years as the
argument from 'trickle down'; the wealth accumulated by the
rich trickles down to the less well off. The security provided by
fixed rights enables the rich to flourish, and in their flourishing they benefit the poor. To some extent, Smith traded on
the thought that the connection between wealth and happiness
was not very direct. The workman relaxing in the sun was as
happy as his master was ever likely to be. Hume supplied
another argument on which Smith sometimes relied to diminish the apparent injustice of the gap between the well being
of rich and poor: wealth had an attractive quality which
disarmed the envy of the poor.[21] Rousseau's picture of society
has the rich grabbing what they can, elbowing aside the poor,
and flaunting their superior well being. Under those conditions it was hard to see the superiority of the rich as anything
other than victory in the class war, a victory secured by
employing the forces of the state to bolster the exploitation
they practised in the economy. Hume and Smith soften the
image; the poor simply see the wealth of the rich as naturally
attached to them, think that their superior lifestyle betokens
superior virtue, and therefore automatically defer to them.
There is no class war, though there is a certain amount of
ideological sleight of hand.

There is no sharp break between the agricultural and the
commercial stages. Rather, once there was fixed property,

commercial progress demanded freedom of contract and liberation from the kind of constraints which landed proprietors like to impose on their successors. Nor was there a uniform connection between property base and political superstructure, though as we have seen, the optimists thought commerce a sound basis for a free representative government and thought any society which was largely populated by a poor peasantry was destined to be governed by absolute monarchs.[22] Historically, there were, of course, numerous different political systems erected on an agricultural foundation, and numerous local variations in what sorts of property were recognized and what rights were held to be part of an owner's rights. So far as law itself went, Roman Law, to take the obvious instance, was not strikingly different under the Empire from what it had been under the Republic; the law which had regulated the affairs of small farmers did not need to envisage new sorts of property right to accommodate the affairs of latifundists farming huge estates under the management of stewards who might well be rich men but were legally slaves. It did need to make ownership more divisible and more flexible, but that did not amount to the discovery of a new conception of property. What always agitated writers who thought in terms of the transition from an agricultural to a commercial society was — as we touched on before — the transition from a society in which 'property' or 'wealth' meant land to one in which they might equally well mean 'money'.[23]

We have seen what this meant for a political theory obsessed by notions of republican virtue. We must consider what it might mean for a more 'sociological' concern. The answer is that it might mean almost anything; what some writers took to be signs of human ingenuity, others took to be evidence of terminal moral decay. The differences between Rousseau and Mandeville provide one instance. Rousseau and Mandeville agreed in much of their sociology, disagreed in what they thought it meant. The buzzing hive described in *The Fable of the Bees* is full of envious, greedy, discontented, and in many ways rather silly creatures; because commerce is a matter of exchange rather than production and profits are made out of changes in taste rather than in satisfying the basic needs of mankind, there is a continuous revolution in tastes going on. Nobody can exactly say the creatures in the hive are happy;

they look over their shoulders to see who is catching them up and look ahead to see whom they are catching up on, and are permanently discontented with what they have already. But the hive prospers; moreover, though the creatures described by Mandeville are not very admirable by the standards of the sternest moralists, they are well adapted to a peaceful and prosperous society.[24]

Rousseau, by contrast, stands with the stern moralist while accepting Mandeville's sociology. What Rousseau deplores is the 'other-directedness' of civilized man. 'Natural man', whom Rousseau identifies with the orang-utan or 'wild man of Borneo' discovered by eighteenth century travellers, was solitary and independent; modern man lives in society but is a slave to the opinion of others. He does not know what he values, what he ought to become, or who he is, save by consulting others. It is public opinion which makes his food taste appetising or disgusting, makes his clothes fashionable or frumpish. Prosperity is no consolation. Modern man is at odds with his fellows. Competition drives him in on himself; he consoles himself with megalomaniac dreams of power over all those who presently humiliate him or render him anxious. So we have a lonely crowd of isolated individuals, who console themselves for their real misery with the pretended goods of a commercial society.[25]

It is evident that none of this lends itself to a very detailed account of the history of property rights. It verges on recapitulating the Christian myth of the Fall; pre-propertied man lived in natural simplicity and harmony, propertied man lives in artificial luxury and disharmony. Unlike the Christian myth, Rousseau's offers no prospect of paradise regained. 'This is hell, nor are we out of it.' Less anxious theorists after Rousseau still agreed with much of his diagnosis. Immanuel Kant admitted that it was an 'unsocial sociability' which drove history; mankind was not born for happiness but for a restless progress.[26] Property must become more and more flexible, more and more usable in the marketplace; mankind must treat their abilities as 'property' if they were to have a motive for developing them. The philosophically minded historian had to trust that all this was progress rather than retrogression.

Hegel, too, absorbed the anxieties of the eighteenth century and tried to place them within an optimistic framework.

Moreover, he did so after an extensive reading in the Scottish economists and historians as well as of philosophers like Kant and Rousseau. Even then, his acceptance of commercial society was half-hearted. Rightly, in view of what was to happen in 1848, Hegel feared that the so-called 'reflective or formal' class — his term for the commercial and professional urban middle class — would be inclined to ask questions of their society which would be corrosive of traditional authority. It was unreasonable to think that men who were forced in earning their livelihood to ask themselves 'is this the most efficient way of achieving my ends?' would refrain from asking the same question of political institutions too.[27]

What did not emerge until well into the 19th Century was any very clear sense that the four stage theory of history needed to be updated and revised to accommodate an industrial stage. There is a good reason for this. If we think in terms of 'forces of production', it is easy to see that the heightened division of labour and the increased pace of innovation which industrialisation brings means a new social stage. An industrial society will require an elaborate commercial life, but will be driven by its industrial engine. The property forms which it requires will not differ very much from those most apt for commerce, however, though every Marxist would insist that their content will change dramatically. Still, the contractual freedom crucial to the one equally suits the other. Nor was it at once obvious that industrialization raised new moral issues. Robert Owen and Thomas Hodgskin denounced the profit of the industrialist as an exploitative deduction from the productive efforts of the worker; but that, after all, was a complaint long directed at the landlord's rent.[28] Indeed, early nineteenth-century capitalists generally managed what they owned, and at least *looked* as if they were doing something to earn their profits.

The one form of ownership which came into its own under industrialism was the joint-stock company with limited liability. Here, too, the possibilities were well understood two centuries earlier; the East India Company was a joint stock trading company which had incidentally acquired the government of a subcontinent. Under an industrial regime, however, the need to assemble much bigger sums of investment capital than were ever needed in previous ages became apparent; the joint stock company was the answer. Its drawback was that if each shareholder was liable for all the debts of the company, the separation of ownership and management which is implied by a joint stock company placed every shareholder at risk of bankruptcy should the managers prove incompetent or criminal. The solution was to limit the liability of each shareholder to the shares he or she bought.

What one might call the social history of property rights as visualized by the eighteenth-century historians is not much affected by all this, however. Their concern with the evolution of property was less to trace the details of legal forms under the economic pressures of new ways of making a living than to draw some sweeping contrasts in the light of the characteristic moral and political debates of their century. In a sense, the point of their histories was to side with or against the noble savage, with or against the nostalgia for Roman virtue and the reckless courage of the Highlander.[29] Because they invented a sociologically fruitful method of conducting this debate, they produced what with hindsight turns out to be an evolutionary theory of some persuasiveness, and because they were able to stand back from the exigencies of the political conflicts of the day, they produced a method of analysis which lends itself to use in other contexts and for other purposes. But — in spite of Marx's enthusiasm for Ferguson — this view of property does not necessarily lead on either to Marx's view of property as alienated labour, nor to the so-called 'economic theory of property rights'. It is too conservative to do the first, too ready to accept the variety of human desires at face value to do the second. As so often in intellectual history, the more closely we scrutinize the concerns of a particular period, the less inclination we feel to reduce them to 'precursors' of later concerns.

The Economic Theory of Property Rights

The economic theory of property rights cannot but remind readers of the utilitarian defence of private property. Utilitarianism justifies private ownership wherever it is an aid to the general happiness, and therefore assesses its merits and defects in terms of its 'efficiency'. Moreover, the utilitarian view of human behaviour associates rationality with utility maximizing in a thoroughly 'economic' way; we each try to maximize the surplus of our happiness over the pains of achieving it, and a rational society organizes itself so as to maximize the surplus of the happiness of all of us over the pains of achieving it.[1]

Utilitarianism, however, is avowedly a normative theory. The economic theory of property rights is at any rate in intention as much an explanatory theory as anything else. It is not only that, and, indeed, its critics generally complain and its defenders deny that it confuses explanation and justification and chronically blurs the line between explanatory and normative concerns.[2] In principle, however, it is perfectly possible to distinguish the two; and the main claim of the theory conceived of as a contribution to explaining how the law is, is that the history of property is the history of increasingly efficient solutions to the problem of economic efficiency. This is, at least, *ceteris paribus*, a justificatory history, but only in the weak sense that it is hard to deny that efficiency is a good thing; it supports, up to a point, the normative claim that the law ought further to improve the system of property rights so as to reap further benefits, although it must be remembered that the more narrowly economic efficiency is defined, the less clear is it that its pursuit either is or should be the be-all and end-all of rational legislation.

Its focus on explanation is not the economic theory's only difference from utilitarianism. Classical utilitarianism takes it for granted that we can compare one person's welfare with another's, and that we can judge someone's actual wants against the wants they *would* have if they were rationally pursuing their own happiness. Like most economists, the defenders of the economic theory of property see the 'economic' assessment of behaviour as purely a matter of efficiency, and therefore of means only. They are not committed to the view that 'utility' in the economist's sense is identical with happiness. Men try to satisfy their wants, but they may want the strangest things. Efficiency is defined in terms of success in satisfying the wants people actually have, and the only test of their having those wants is the choices they make when they are offered them in a marketplace. Efficiency is maximized when resources are in the hands of those who would pay most for them. And, in the words of the author of *The Economic Analysis of Law*, one of the basic economic concepts 'is the tendency of resources to gravitate towards their most valuable uses if voluntary exchange — a market — is permitted.'[3]

Enthusiasts for the economic theory of property rights happily acknowledge their debts to Smith, Hume — even to Sir William Blackstone; the proposition that no man will sow where another will reap founds the general case for recognizing property rights at all.[4] The suggestion thereafter is that communal property or a 'no-ownership' system will give way to private property if there is an effective means of replacing less efficient forms of ownership with more efficient. The inefficiency of communal property is often argued by reference to 'the tragedy of the commons'. Suppose we are villagers who communally possess a common pasture on which we may graze our cows, without payment, because nobody has rights over the pasture which add up to property in it. Since we do not have to pay for grazing a cow, we do not have to take into account the real cost of doing so — which is the burden each extra cow imposes on all graziers. If someone else adds a cow to the herd, there will be less grass for our cows, but we have no way of stopping them. Indeed, our answer will probably be to add another cow ourselves, since we will be better off with two skinny cows than one skinny cow. Add together all our defensive efforts, and the common pasture will be grazed to dust and we shall all starve. We have each imposed the external costs of our grazing on everyone else, and the result is disaster. If the land had been privately owned and the right to graze a cow let out to each of us, the owner of the land would have had an incentive to allow only the 'optimal' number of cows to graze — because each cow above that number would have diminished the rent paid by the rest of us, and each cow below that number would have reduced the total rent the owner could have got, and would thus have given him an incentive to add one more. His ownership allows us to be charged the full social cost of grazing our cows.[5]

The argument is less a decisive argument for *private* property than an argument for placing everything of value in the hands of somebody who is in a position to charge for its use and has an incentive to charge the full economic price.[6] Here we might envisage a 'private' solution if each of us could charge the others for the costs their adding another cow would impose, or a 'public' solution if the whole plot were owned by someone who could impose such charges. It is possible to construct an analogous case to that of the tragedy of the commons, where private property in the usual sense exists but where the incentives to individuals ensure that the outcome is sub-optimal. (This, incidentally, is part of any sensible reply to complaints that the economic analysis of law is necessarily conservative, procapitalist, pro-big business or whatever. It leaves wide open the question whether a private or public solution is (normatively) preferred or (as a matter of fact) the more likely to emerge.) Suppose we all own a little plot of land, and that on our land are trees which are individually valuable to each of us as firewood, but which serve an even more useful public purpose in preventing soil erosion. The prevention of soil erosion, however, is a collective good in the sense that it is no use my preserving my two trees except as part of a screen; if the screen comes down anyway, I am better off using my trees for firewood than having an inadequate screen and no firewood. The odds are that we shall cut down our trees and suffer soil erosion. Cutting down my trees will do little to cause soil erosion if they are the only ones to come down, and leaving them uncut will do nothing to stop it if they are the only ones not to come down. Either way, I might as well use them for firewood. Only if we can somehow coordinate our response in such a way as to charge the person cutting down their trees the full cost of their contribution to the erosion of the soil will the outcome be efficient in the sense of ensuring that all resources are used to produce maximum utility.

What is needed is some way of charging each of us the full social cost of our trees; unless somebody can do that, the fact that we own our individual plots in a way that nobody owned portions of the common makes no difference. What, in this scenario, nobody 'owns' is the right to forbid others to cause soil erosion. The economic theory of property rights, viewed as a contribution to the history of property essentially invites us to consider the history of property as the history of attempts to reconcile private ownership and overall efficiency. In general, the thought is that giving people property rights in anything of value is the best way of ensuring that resources are used as efficiently as possible. It is an empirical observation that parks are more littered than private gardens, that simple societies without private ownership do more damage to their land than complex, private propertied societies, that centrally planned, publicly owned economies such as that of the Soviet Union are inefficient in giving consumers what they want, and no better than economies based on private property so far as pollution, public health, job satisfaction and the rest are concerned.

The theory tells us something of why this should be so. Suppose I am growing corn alongside a railway line; the railway company would like to run its (steam powered) trains at 90 mph, but at that speed they would emit tremendous quantities of sparks and destroy my crops. At 75 mph they would have only a one in five chance of so doing. At 40 mph, they would not do it at all. If the railway company is simply forbidden to run its trains at more than 40 mph my crops are saved, but the passengers travel slower than they want, and the railway's revenue falls as they lose passengers who would travel with them if the trains were fast and will not travel with them if they go more slowly. If the railway company may scatter its sparks where it likes, I suffer disaster as my livelihood goes up in smoke. What we cannot tell, in the absence of a market in the right to cause emissions is what is the most efficient solution.[7]

A famous essay by Richard Coase, from which the example comes, explains how all can be cured by creating a property right in spark emission. Suppose the farmer would lose £500 if his crops were burnt; anything more the £500 would compensate him for trains going past at 90 mph, and a little more than £100 would compensate him for trains going past at 75 mph — he could insure himself against a one in five risk for a little more than £100. If the right to allow or forbid the emissions is in the hands of the farmer, the railway has to decide whether the benefit to it of running its trains at 90 mph rather than 75 mph is worth more than £400, and whether the benefit to it of running its trains at 75 mph rather than 40 mph is worth more than £100. If the extra revenue from the speed loving passengers was £2,000 and the farm the only problem, then the railway company will happily pay up; if there are several farmers, they may settle for 75 mph trains and lower charges from the farmers. If there is no mutually agreeable outcome, it suggests the railway ought not to be built.

This solution will only be reached in practice if there are no 'transaction costs', that is, no costs in making and going through with the agreement to transfer the right to make sparks. One reason why the idea of giving people property rights in other people's grazing or tree-cutting looks such an implausible solution to over-grazing or soil erosion is that in real life the 'transaction costs' of getting us to use those rights would be very high. Even as pure theory the solution implausibly requires that people's wants are unrelated to their incomes or wealth. Moreover, the transaction must be isolated from other transactions — it may be 'efficient' for the railroad to burn one farmer's crops with impunity, but not if it puts everyone off farming. Given these implausibilities, all that matters for efficiency is that *someone* should own the right to burn the crops; it does not matter who. Total benefit remains the same whether the farmer has to buy the railway company's forbearance or the railway company has to buy the risk to the farmer's crop. If the ability to go at 90 mph is worth more than the unburnt crops, then trains should go at that speed, and if not, not. Who has to buy off whom depends on the initial allocation of rights; for economic efficiency, it does not matter which way round the rights have been allocated. Most students of the subject flinch at this claim, since they dislike the thought that poor farmers may have to pay rich railroads not to burn their crops; but efficiency in the economist's sense has nothing to do with justice. The initial distribution of title to resources is a matter for our notions of justice or propriety or whatever else we bring to bear. Economics is professionally unconcerned.[8]

If this idea is plausible — it plainly is, since it is only a restatement of the basic ideas of Pareto-efficiency — we still have to link it to the thought that there will be a pressure to create such all embracing systems of property rights. We cannot suppose that such pressure is always successful, since we know many societies in which the tragedy of the commons is enacted. Nor can we suppose that property rights in everything of value will have emerged as the solution wherever tragedy does not occur. It may be that the tragedy of the commons is averted by customary rights which allow some elder of the village to dictate the cow population of the pasture without having anything recognizable as ownership — he may have the right to dictate grazing levels and none of the other elements of the *jus utendi et abutendi*. Trees may survive because they are held to be sacred, and not vulnerable to being cut down for firewood.

Enthusiasts for the economic analysis of social behaviour may well want to explain such forms of behaviour and such rights in functional terms, as ways of achieving the same sort of efficiency as the invention of property rights. The plausibility of this project is not something we need to consider here; we are interested in the evolution of property rights in particular. An evolutionary story may persuade us that the need to promote efficient use of resources at least puts some pressure on all institutions and practices without persuading us that property rights will emerge as the favoured solution in all cases. That would be a victory for a weak economic theory. To support a strong economic interpretation of the history of property, we should need to show that the property rights solution to problems of resource allocation is more efficient than any of its near-equivalents, and that social pressures for efficiency are so intense that it is the most efficient solution which will emerge.

There is a case for saying that of all the the possible solutions, that which gives people property in things of value —

things always being taken to include such 'things' as the licence to broadcast on a certain frequency or to emit smoke of a certain degree of obnoxiousness or whatever — is uniquely efficient and uniquely stable.[9] It does not suffer from what all the other solutions do suffer from, namely vulnerability to erosion as society secularizes. The elder gets his authority only because we believe that age brings wisdom or sanctity; that belief absent, his capacity to solve the problem of how to use the commons enough but not too much has gone. Trees protected only by superstition will not last longer than the superstition. Moreover, as 'individualism' in all its various senses becomes central to the moral, legal and political culture, so a view of law as naturally adapted to the facilitation and enforcement of individually made bargains is likely to grow too — the process described in Maine's classic history as the change 'from status to contract'.[10]

Moreover, there is much in legal history which seems to be explained in the way the theory suggests. The familiar mortgage took a long time to gain acceptance by the courts, and until it did, it was difficult to raise money on the security of landed property. The process followed a familiar pattern. Individuals made informal bargains and tried to get the courts to recognize them; eventually, case law hardened into law solid enough to bind lenders and borrowers.[11] If the railway and the farmer began in a legal framework which treated the issue as a matter for the criminal law, making it an offence to emit sparks or to interfere with the railway, we can see without much trouble how either side might try to buy off the other. The railway might pay the farmer not to complain to the authorities, or the farmer might see what the railway would charge not to use the freedom the law secured to it. Since nothing morally important hung on it, we should hardly see any reason to interfere with such transactions. A property right in spark emission would simply formalize that process.

The evolution of property rights then becomes a history of how pressures towards efficiency do or do not make themselves felt. One obvious area of interest is the history of slavery. In the case of the slave states of the USA in the early nineteenth-century, many commentators held at the time that free labour was really cheaper than slave labour and that economic progress would abolish slavery — the costs of production with free labour were lower in proportion to the value of output than the costs of production with slave labour, because slave labour was very unproductive. But no erosion of the institution of property in living persons occurred. There have been various explanations offered; one, put forward in *Time on the Cross* denied that slavery was as inefficient as all previous observers had supposed, but it carried only partial conviction. Although it rested on some impressive econometric evidence, it seemed to some critics to rest on the proposition it was supposed to support, that people generally choose the most efficient means of achieving their goals.[12] The more plausible view is that there were cultural forces which subverted the search for efficiency and prevented the erosion of slavery. For instance, in a society where manual labour is done by slaves, the association of work and servility is likely to inhibit free labourers from looking for work; where management consists of making a slave gang work in the fields, it is unlikely that the sort of management required for getting the best out of free labour will be easy to find. Then, one has to reckon with the fact that 'efficiency' in the narrow sense of maximizing the surplus of revenues over costs may be at odds with the enjoyment of the aristocratic and leisured life to which the slave owners aspired. Perhaps slavery was 'efficient' in realising wishes which 'efficient' people would not have had.[13]

The eventual demise of slavery suggests a mechanism which would explain the replacement of less efficient property rights with more efficient ones — the strains, direct and indirect, of competition with other states. The southern states of the union were unable to compete with the northern states; in many places it was cheaper to import northern foodstuffs than to produce their own, it was impossible to sustain southern-based transport undertakings against northern ones — though it must be said that once the northerners got a monopoly of provision, they rigged their charges too, which reflected monopoly power rather than efficiency. It was in fact the Civil War which put an end to slavery, but the strains and stresses which caused the Civil War were themselves due to the slave states' inability to compete with the non-slave states. So we may assert as a general rule that where a more and a less efficient system come into competition, there will be a tendency for the more efficient practices to replace the less efficient. Slavery was conquered out of existence because it failed to sell out, and refused to copy its rivals.[14]

The truth of any such explanation is a question of history. But the plausibility of the economic theory of property is reinforced by the naturalness of our inclination to ask, not 'why did they resort to more efficient forms of ownership?' but 'why did they not?' There are, however, four things one ought to observe about the economic theory, two harmless to it, and two not. The first is that 'efficiency' may often not be an overriding moral value, either for us or for the people whose behaviour we are explaining. It is sometimes complained of by extreme enthusiasts for coordination by ownership that the absence of property rights in our own bodily parts diminishes efficiency. If I could raise money by selling a couple of fingers from my left hand, it might well be a good bargain to do so. If I could sell the right to use bits of myself for spare parts surgery after my death, I could now raise money on what would eventually be of no use to me, thus increasing the efficiency with which human bodies are used. Judges have generally resisted any move in this direction, insisting that bodies are *nullum in bonis*, and that it would be *contra bonos mores* to recognize property in them. In English law, this has the result that it is impossible to steal a body, and that if a body is removed from the control of an executor of a will — as the body of an IRA hunger-striker was once taken by the IRA in the hope of giving it a military funeral — the executor is entitled to a possessory injunction to allow the body burial, but to nothing more. Mortuary attendants who remove the pancreas from corpses in their care cannot be accused of stealing them, though they certainly do something they are not entitled to do.[15]

The critic who dislikes the thought of the human body being fully-fledged property and is therefore not moved by the thought that bodies would be used more efficiently if they fully owned often has two distinct objections in mind. The first is a pure moral objection. It is simply disgusting, obnoxious or otherwise to be deplored if bodily parts are made the objects of commercial transactions. How far, we may ask rhetorically, is it to go? If you have a taste for fingers and offer me enormous sums for mine, is this to pass without comment? The answer, strictly in terms of the theory, is yes. If all wants are equal and efficiency is a matter of maximally gratifying wants then no holds are barred. But it is entirely possible, both for explanatory and for normative purposes, to bracket away the demands of morality. As an explanatory theory, we are left with the thought that property rights will over a long run reflect the pressures of the effective satisfaction of what a given society recognises as 'licit' wants. As a normative theory we are left with the claim that unmade bargains which would increase the sum of satisfactions of licit wants will be made if we invent property rights to facilitate their being made. Persons who contemplate garage sales of surplus organs can then be fought off on the question of whether a market in such things is too morally dreadful to contemplate.[16]

The second objection is less a matter of an intuitive dislike of dealing in what ought not to be dealt in than distaste for the injustice of the bargains which are struck. Often what critics have in mind is the nastiness of a world in which, say, corneas are bought from poor Indians by rich Americans. That one good eye and £2,000 is worth more to a starving man than two good eyes and £0.00 is not in question. It is the way the initial distributions of income and wealth distort the bargaining positions of the two parties which upsets observers, or the way poverty may 'force' us to part with something we ought not to. Once again, the economic theory of property rights can bracket out considerations of justice and injustice. As explanation, all it says is that the way property rights have developed and the way they have been transferred from one man to another is at any rate frequently best explained by the need to make the most efficient use of resources. It is, so to speak, not the theory's business if some people have very few resources and some people have a lot. There will be innumerable cases which will strike the moralist as painfully as the sale of corneas. The poor will have less safe airports than the rich, but so they should. If they have fewer resources altogether, efficiency is not promoted by their spending so much on safety that they have nothing left to spend on transport.[17] Normatively, the theory starts with resources as they are distributed and discusses the most efficient use to which they can be put. It is open to anyone to say that they would rather discuss the question of that initial distribution. The objection to the Indian beggar selling his cornea to a rich American is not to the sale of the cornea as such, nor to the proposition that the beggar is quite right to prefer one eye and the money to two eyes and no money; the objection is to the distribution of assets which makes his choice a rational one. On that the theory is silent. What it is not silent on is the thought that once we have a satisfactory distribution of initial holdings efficiency is promoted by free transfers.[18]

If complaints about justice are satisfactorily dealt with, a complaint from within the theory's own premises is perhaps harder to deal with. This is the objection that the theory does not allow for the risk that people will be tempted to use their property rights in a non-efficiency promoting way. Suppose I have a large sum of money which I invest in a piece of land near a pretty residential area. I announce that I am going to build a tannery. I then invite the residents to buy off this potential nuisance. It may well be that were I to run a tannery I could make £30,000 a year profit, and that the residents will pay me £40,000 a year not to run my tannery — so I pocket the £40,000. I then go and do the same a few miles away, and in effect blackmail one area after another into buying off this threatened nuisance.[19]

There are examples of such behaviour in the most sophisticated markets of all, namely on stock exchanges. Companies have been forced to reorganize their finances and even alter their whole way of working in order to buy off a predatory bidder who is far from wishing to take over the enterprise and make it more profitable. He sees that if he purchases shares and is thought to be about to make a bid, the price will rise and he can take a profit. He never needs to make a full-scale bid (though recent legislation tries to force him to do so), only to threaten to make one. So long as it is known that he could do it, and so long as there is some idea of what the prospective profit might be, the price for getting rid of him is known. It is very noticeable that all the examples relied on by enthusiasts for an economic analysis of legal institutions presuppose that some plausible productive purpose is in question — growing corn and transporting passengers are good examples of productive purposes which happen to be in competition when the railway runs past your farm. Blackmailing activities do not fit the model; or rather, it takes some intellectual heroism to try to legitimate even blackmail as a matter of selling something

— viz, secrecy — to the person who values it most highly.[20]

It is quite difficult to find a general criterion for productive as opposed to unproductive transfers. That we want such a criterion is clear enough; trains at 75 mph and a one in five danger of crop destruction is very arguably better than slow trains and safe crops or very fast trains and no crops, while your money in my pocket and no tannery anywhere is at best no better than your money in your pocket and no tannery anywhere. If we are to believe that the history of property rights is the history of efficiency, we must also believe that the demands of efficiency *in a morally reputable sense* are so obvious that legislatures and law courts are unlikely to take long to stamp out abuses. The filter mechanisms that let in virtuous uses will also filter out vicious ones.

Lastly, however, we come to an objection which bites harder. If we separate out the normative and explanatory uses of the economic theory of ownership, we may come to cast doubt therefore on the normative of 'wants' and power of 'efficiency'. It is not that there is nothing to be said for the thought that adequate property rights and a well run market place allow resources to be put to their best use, it is rather that there is not enough to be said for it to support either historical optimism or a normative theory of law. In some situations, 'private' solutions work badly; 'public goods' which may include clean air, national defence, safety devices like light-houses and many more, and which *ex hypothesi* do not allow for the exclusion of anyone from using them, cannot be supplied by the market place trading in private property. More-over, persons who are unable to reach a 'public goods' solution to a problem will adjust their wants and their behav-iour to what they can have. So the wants which are efficiently met by the market place and by owners coordinating their activities by transferring property rights are not rock bottom wants built into human nature but wants which are already contaminated (for normative purposes) by the environment in which they are operating.[21]

This might be thought to leave the explanatory aspect of the economic theory untouched, and here it is this aspect with which we are mainly concerned. However, the 'normative' scepticism of the last paragraph has a natural concomitant in scepticism about the implications of appeals to efficiency when it comes to writing history. On the one hand, it may lead writers to represent all previous ages as efficiently organized for whatever they were efficiently organized for, which is the ultimate in vapidity; on the other, it may lead writers to ignore the extent to which social, legal and political change has taken place not as a quiet evolutionary process of increasing efficiency in the use of resources, but under the impact of greed, violence, and revolutionary upheaval. There is, of course, no necessary connection between the idea that legal changes take place in the direction of greater efficiency and the idea that they do so quietly. As Hume observed, force and fraud are the origins of most governments, even if their subsequent existence is an absolutely blameless record of public good. None the less, if one puts together a scepticism about the extent to which coordination via property and the marketplace is efficient and a scepticism about the degree to which history proceeds under the impulsion of a deliberate quest for efficiency in the first place, one result may be Marx's theory of history. For here we have a history in which the productive effectiveness of both equipment and labour is constantly enhanced, but where the gap between individual good and social good never narrows, and 'efficiency' in the sense of satisfying the most important human needs is never achieved this side of socialism, and where progress is achieved only through violent upheaval culminating in the abolition of property rights altogether.

Property, Progress and Alienation

Marx was deeply indebted both to the ideas implicit in the economic theory of property and to the anthropology of the eighteenth-century Scottish historians. He felt more kinship with the second than with the first, because he thought that almost all economic theories were surreptitiously justificatory — in particular, they suggested that human nature was always what it was in capitalist nineteenth-century Britain and that the present economic order was therefore the crowning achievement of human rationality. In the face of squalor, misery, overwork and 'the anarchy of capitalist production' this was too much to stomach. On the other hand, he did not deny that capitalist property relations were the most efficient yet devised, viewed from the perspective of trying to get the maximum production out of men and materials. The Scottish emphasis on the unintended consequences of social interaction, and their insistence on tempering any static analysis with a sensitivity to the differences made by historical change, however, was much more sympathetic as methodology.[1]

What he added to these ingredients altered their complexion entirely. This was a Hegelian vision of human history as the history of freedom, but couched in terms entirely opposed to Hegel's own. Hegel, starting and ending as a philosopher, saw freedom as the fruit of knowledge. History as such was the process by which Spirit or the inherent rationality of the world came to full self-consciousness and brought the world into a satisfactory reflection of that self-consciousness. To put it vulgarly, history was the autobiography of God, and God's work was the creation of a free world. 'For the History of the World is nothing but the development of the idea of Freedom

. . . . Philosophy concerns itself only with the glory of the Idea mirroring itself in the History of the World.'[2] Human institutions were one face of this process: 'the State is the March of God on Earth'.[3] So for Hegel, property reflected the right of mankind to dominate and master mere nature; initially rights were collective and tribal, so property was collective. Now, however, we could see that freedom was a matter of individual self-expression, and so property was essentially individual property. As we saw when discussing 'personalist' theories of property, this view is wholly consistent with an emphasis on the social nature of individuality. It is not because I am *me*, a bare atom, that I claim individual sovereignty over what counts as my property, but because I am husband, father, doctor and citizen, and in these roles realize myself as an individual.[4]

Hegel's account has an obvious historical link to the eighteenth-century Scots; they saw modern society as so to speak peaking in the commercial and industrial world of the late eighteenth-century, and Hegel put a philosophical gloss on their data. It also picks up much that the economic theory would pick up; modern man is concerned to be efficient, is interested in means-end rationality in a way primitive man was not and tradition based societies are not. Unlike them, Hegel was frightened of the corrosive effects of instrumental rationality. But his solution to these anxieties outraged Marx and set him off on a distinctive and disconcerting approach to history.[5]

Hegel held that we could be anchored in our societies if we were attached by law, opinion and belief to particular social roles and social positions. Individual traders would be dangerous men unless they belonged to corporations devoted to the public good, and unless the state could set prices and wages and conditions of work. Equally, forms of property such as entailed estates would be obsolete restrictions on individuality unless they served a useful purpose. Happily they did serve such a purpose. Landowners who could not buy or sell their own or other men's estates, but who lived where their forbears lived, did what they did, and thought as they thought, provided a counterweight to the lighter-minded urban professionals. There would be an agrarian culture of a sober, conservative and slow moving kind which would lend stability to the existing order. How could we know that this balance was what constituted freedom? By means of Hegel's philosophy, which assures us that the Idea realizes itself in such a balanced diversity of institutional arrangements.[6]

Marx hated this doctrine. It tried to persuade us that all the conflict and misery of the real world were illusions; and it was not even coherent in itself. It made out that property was essentially an expression of individual mastery of the world, and then proceeded to put all its trust in a form of property which was absolutely not under individual control, namely entailed landed property. None the less, it contained the clue to the truth about property. This was that property was at one and the same time the object of human freedom and the external force which tyrannized over us. Hegel was right to see that the key to history was freedom; he was right to see that freedom essentially involved human mastery of the world. He was even right in thinking that the key to unfreedom was the concept of alienation. He made three great mistakes however.[7]

The first was to think that we had attained freedom. On the contrary, under capitalism we were utterly unfree. Indeed we were paradoxically more entirely dominated by capital than the slave was ever dominated by his master — though Marx was careful not to say that we were worse off than the slave had been. The second was to think that men, individually and socially, mastered the world through their ownership of property. On the contrary, it owned us. It was not through property but through its abolition that we could really come to possess the world. Until we overcame the illusions of property things would continue to master men. Thirdly, Hegel's conception of the overcoming of alienation was entirely intellectual. He visualized us coming to be at home in the world solely as a result of our understanding the world. Hegel's solution was Idealist because the problem he set himself was one to which an Idealist solution was relevant, indeed the only one possible. For Hegel the world was 'alien' only because we could not see how a world of independent matter could be the world grasped by thought. Once we saw that it was really the invention of Mind, we were reconciled. Nonsense, thought Marx; reconciliation was out of the question. It was a real, material world, and what was wanted was its recapture by those who had really created it, namely labouring humanity.[8]

The argument can be very complicated, but its essence is not. Mankind began more or less at the mercy of nature. In one way, this was the stage of maximum alienation or unfreedom, when we had very few forces of our own with which to control and exploit nature. What happened to us was what nature did to us. But the course of history is the course of increasingly effective technology. Contrary to many commentators, Marx offers no real theory of what makes technology improve; it certainly is not a matter of individual striving after efficiency, since Marx insists that that is not part of our natural endowment. Techniques will not work themselves, so we must have some system of rights to the use and enjoyment of things in order for production to take place and anyone to know what is his or hers to consume. In all this Marx generally follows the Scottish historians. Private property, marriage, state institutions and social classes come on the scene together. The state enables the possessors of property to exploit the non-possessors, whether this is via direct slavery or serfdom or landlordism or capitalist employment. It enforces the property rights on which exploitation depends.[9]

More importantly, at least for our concerns, a society so constituted turns into an entity propelled by natural forces — or what are for all intents and purposes natural forces — whose operations are no part of anyone's purposes. The more developed the forms of property and the more perfect the market the less any actual person can decide what is to happen in the world, and the more it is decided by things. This is not, of course, to be taken literally. My factory does not literally start itself up at 7 am on Monday morning, whatever I may do to prevent it. Rather, I am faced with a world in which my factory merely represents a certain stock of capital, and one in which I have to maximize the return on my capital or perish. I might like to produce gold plated widgets, but if the demand is for aluminium plated ones, that settles it. I might like my workmen individually, but if demand for my product drops, I shall have to get rid of them, get into a new line of business and take on different employees. It is obvious that they, the propertyless have no freedom of choice; they must work or starve. It is true up to a point that they may choose whom to work for, but in a perfect market all employers must treat them in exactly the same way. Unlike the slave who at least could hope to run away and if he remained free for a year and a day shed his servile status, the worker can never get out of the shadow of capital.[10] Neither can the owner, who is obviously better fed, and in some senses freer than his employees and yet in others just as much the slave of capital as they are.

This vision is explicit only in Marx's youthful writings and to a limited extent in his unpublished *Grundrisse*. But it forms a background to his entire social and economic theory. As one might expect, the vision of mankind at the mercy of social forces they have unleashed without understanding them has its corollary in a theory of historical change in which exploitation and violent revolution play the causative role and in which progress towards a future of rational self-direction is only a by-product of mankind's actual intentions.

Property begins in slavery. There is a throwaway suggestion that the differentiation of men and women is the beginning of the division of labour and that women are the first slaves, but the more consistent view is that property begins with the violent seizing of slaves by those with the physical force or military prowess to seize them. Even when simply following Ferguson's chronicle of the movement from the ownership of bows and furs to the ownership of waggons and flocks, Marx emphasizes the role of cupidity and violence.[11]

Thereafter, we have what we might predict. Classes form either to exploit their power over the less advantaged or to resist those who would exploit them. Although power depends in the end on a class's value to the development of the productive forces, no ruling class will retire gracefully upon learning that there are more efficient ways of organizing production than those from which it has benefitted. It can only be swept away by a new class with a burning sense of grievance against the existing order and the capacity to dominate the new order. Social evolution proceeds by means of political revolution. This process does not occur everywhere; some societies violate the linear scheme of a progress from primitive communism through ancient, feudal and bourgeois capitalist societies to the final destination of mature communism. 'The Asiatic Mode of Production' fails to generate any social change, has no revolutions — though it has lots of palace coups which change the governing personnel without changing the nature of the political system — and seems not to have classes in the sense we know them in the west.[12]

The readiness with which Marx introduces cases which will not fit his simple linear model of transformation suggests that he may not have intended to commit himself to the existence of one path only. We may understand him better if we understand him to be claiming only that the linear process has a simple logic which illuminates both the cases which fit it most readily and the cases which do not. These latter are to be understood as cases where a 'natural' process has become in one way or another blocked or diverted. We can see that the linear process is the natural process not by looking at it with ethno-centric European eyes but by realizing that no society would autonomously return from the later stages to the earlier and that whenever a European society at a 'later' stage comes into contact with a society at an earlier stage, it is the latter which gives way. It is not only the guns of the soldiers of the East India Company which enable the very small numbers of British conquerors to seize and govern the Indian sub-continent, it is habits of application, powers of social organization, the ability to calculate costs and apply maximum resources at the right moment. No wonder Marx sees it as battering down the walls of barbarian indifference.[13]

So, we have a vision which is simultaneously a historical sketch and a moral drama. The historical process is — as Hegel said — a 'slaughterbench', not the working out of a calm calculation. It is driven by the basest forces, not a philosophical ideal. It has under capitalism reached the height of paradox. We have the most powerful incentives constantly to revolutionize the forces of production, not because we have any interest in enabling mankind to do so, but because we shall go bankrupt if we do not keep up. It is a moral drama, because we are the unwitting agents of a greater purpose than our own, and because the search for freedom takes place under the most coercive impulses.

Moreover, whichever way we turn the story we find the same mixture of empirical paradox and underlying purpose. Capitalism demands of workers and employers alike that they acquire new skills; but it simultaneously cheapens every skill and makes employers sack expensive skilled workers in order to replace them with cheaper unskilled ones. It encourages innovations in consumption as well as production in order to keep up output and profit.[14] But it simultaneously forces producers to simplify their products to get the benefit of extended production. We thus live in a world where the liberation of our ownership of things from all sorts of traditional ties and from all sorts of moral restraint means that things diversify and simplify as if under their own will, making us gain and lose new abilities as if we were their playthings.

The world of consumption displays the same paradoxes as the world of production. The poverty of the worker means that he is enslaved by his needs. He works because 'he has to'; he would starve if he did not, and may well go hungry even if he gets work. Hunger of itself is no bad thing; if we did not have to eat we would have no occasion to socialize over the supper table, and life would be much duller. But to be forced to do an intolerable job by the need to eat is to be the victim of the material world. Given the horrors of capitalism, it is a misfortune to have any needs whatever — all of them make one vulnerable to the need for money, and therefore drive one into the marketplace where as Marx says the worker has nothing to take to market but his hide and will not escape without a tanning.[15]

As if this were not enough, the habits of consumption themselves show the alienating impact of capitalism. The rich man buys a painting. Is he really 'appropriating' the object he has purchased? Marx denies it. A painting is only a painting in virtue of being the expression of the aesthetic insights and expressive skills of the artist. To appropriate it is to be able to incorporate within oneself the skills that went into it. The rich man who buys such things commonly does so to demonstrate his wealth. It is like putting a large cheque on the wall. As Marx cynically suggests, 'are you ugly, send your money courting for you'; it is simultaneously true that money can get you whatever you want and false. The educated ear can really appropriate the symphony in the way the uneducated ear cannot. Wealth, and the ownership of things brings us no nearer real appropriation.[16]

So we get a vision of a world in which production is dictated by the accidents of market interaction based on individual ownership of labour power and other productive forces. Such a world is one in which individuals can in a sense do what they like with what they own, and in another sense have no choice about what to like to do with them. As Marx always insisted, none of this was to accuse capitalists of behaving badly; they were simply 'bearers of capitalist relations'. They could honestly say that they were forced to do what they did. Were they to pay more than their competitors they would be bankrupt; there was no room for individual benevolence no matter what they felt. If production is so dictated so must consumption be. What is produced only minimally reflects human needs, for what it must reflect is the need to maximize exchange value in order to maximize capital accumulation.

Similarly work is dictated both as to length and as to technique by the demands of capital accumulation. Instead of work expressing human creativity and imagination, it is forced labour, grinding toil, which as Marx says men flee like the devil as soon as they are able. In a really human society work would be a form of human communication as well as a necessity for satisfying our needs in the usual limited sense. I would see the objects I made as valuable because they met your needs; you would see my work as valuable because it met your needs. We should reinforce the regard we felt for each other by working together for one another's benefit.[17] As it is, I grudgingly produce what I hope will make money for me, and care nothing for the benefit it may do you. Our products compete with each other, are in essence each other's enemies. How can they be at war with each other and their producers not be? It is, to repeat, not because we are naturally inclined to be at odds with each other that society is based on this war of all against all. It is because our social interaction is governed by the demands of our property, not rationally organized for the benefit of us all.

This brings us to the crux. Is there some sort of propertyless realm of freedom which we shall secure under socialism? It is a familiar and wholly justified complaint against Marx that he never said anything extended or detailed about the organization of socialism. He was eloquent in denouncing the horrors of capitalism, but reticent about the rest. We know that there will be neither law nor government, police nor ideology under socialism. There therefore cannot be property in the sense with which we are familiar with it. Doubtless individuals will be able to rely on access to the goods they wish to use and consume — clothes, housing, books and so on; but it will not be secured by the law. There will have to be some system or other enabling production to be coordinated and directed; so someone or some group or institution must be able to rely on exercising control over materials, machinery and labour. But it will not be by way of legally certified ownership.

As to what it will be, silence falls. Moreover, silence falls among Marx's followers too. It is obvious enough that socialism as practised has universally required some sort of public ownership in a form familiar from the context of private ownership. That is, officials and administrators have legally guaranteed rights to control and dispose of assets held in freehold by the state, or by some entity constituted by legislative action. The workers in industries owned by the state have not usually had any more say in how they are run and what they produce than under capitalism. Conversely, where they have had some say as in Yugoslav experiments with workers' cooperatives, there have been the same problems with booms and slumps, fluctuations in profit and employment, as under capitalism. In neither form of common ownership has there been any sign of people adopting wholly different attitudes to consumption from those they have under capitalism.[18]

Marxian freedom is tempting because we have something of the sense he has of the paradoxes of social life. We know that we have complete liberty to choose our employers, but also that we may have to settle for something far different from what we should wish to do with our working lives. We are sharply aware of the contrast between the detailed control and management we can individually bring to our lives and the chaotic way a whole economy operates. We are equally aware of the contrast between what we happen to want at present and what we might desire if we were more relaxed, better educated, more at ease with one another. Marx never dreamed that capitalism could become as prosperous as it has in fact become; but even the cheerfullest capitalist occasionally wonders whether all his wants are expressions of a fulfilled and autonomous character or whether a number are not so to speak attempts at consolation for the unsatisfactoriness of a competitive society.

If it is tempting, it is still not an entirely coherent vision of freedom. How we are to be both entirely free as individuals and entirely free as a society in charge of its own productive activities is impossible to spell out. Moreover, the Marxist emphasis on complete freedom, which sees property as nothing but a drag on our choices, makes two mistakes which weaken it a good deal. In the first place, Marx underestimates the good that property can do. If there was no ownership in the usual sense, there would be less room for expressions of friendship, for voluntarily giving to others what we do not have to. We do not need property to go out of our way to be kind, to pay particular attention to others and so on. We do, however, need rights of some sort. Unless we do what we have the right not to do, there is no question of gratitude; yet Marx's own account of the value of fulfilling work depends upon our feeling mutual gratitude while expressing utter hostility to all talk of rights.[19] Moreover, some of these rights must be rights over things as well as over our own behaviour. Ownership as we know it might be much attenuated, but unless individuals retain control of the fate of particular objects, there will be a severely reduced scope for generosity — at any rate as we value it. Marx does not envisage a new tribalism. Again, he wants us to realize our full individuality; that also requires control over things that display our tastes and talents. Something like property rights over consumables is needed if there is to be a community of individuals; without individuality, the notion of freedom hardly makes sense as a moral goal.

Turning away from freedom, there may also be more to be said for the disciplining and anchoring effects of property than Marx ever admitted. Indeed, that thought may equally cast doubt on Marx's conception of freedom. To have sufficient character to be a stable person at all seems to involve discipline as well as mere licence; in fact, without some constraints it is hard to see what freedom would be freedom to do. It may be that Rousseau and Hegel were nearer the truth than Marx; property and freedom are connected, not in the sense that the abolition of property is the condition of freedom, but in the sense that freedom for us needs a mixture of endowment and anchorage, and any society's property institutions reflect less the achievement of liberty or the culmination of slavery than the temporary balance it has struck between a plurality of ambitions. There is no Golden Age behind or before us, only endless argument and experiment.

Notes

Introduction

1. Kenneth Minogue, 'The Concept of Property and Its Contemporary Significance', in *Nomos*, XXII, pp. 3–5.
2. *Anarchy, State and Utopia*, pp. 158ff.
3. H.L.A. Hart, 'Prolegomenon to the Principles of Punishment', *Proceedings of the Aristotelian Society*, pp. 1– 26.
4. John Rawls, *A Theory of Justice*, Oxford University Press, 1971.
5. F.A. von Hayek, *Law, Legislation and Liberty*, vol. II.
6. *Anarchy, State and Utopia*, ch. 7.
7. I. Hont and M. Ignatieff, eds, *Wealth and Virtue*.

Chapter 1

1. G.E.M. de Ste Croix, *Class Struggle in the Ancient Greek World*, p. 44.
2. Aristotle, *Politics*, Book V, pp. 237ff.
3. Alfred Zimmern, *The Greek Commonwealth*, p. 133.
4. *Greek Commonwealth*, pp. 180–89.
5. Plato, *The Republic*, pp. 174–5.
6. *Republic*, p. 106.
7. *Greek Commonwealth*, pp. 287–8.
8. *Republic*, pp. 63ff.
9. Niccolo Macchiavelli, *The Prince and the Discourses*, p. 152.
10. *Republic*, pp. 63ff.
11. ibid., p. 106.
12. Karl Popper, *The Open Society and Its Enemies*, v. 1, pp. 157ff.
13. Gabriel Klosko, *Plato's Political Thought*, pp. 210–11.
14. Plato, *The Laws*, p. 363.
15. Sheldon Wolin,. *Politics and Vision*, pp. 62–5.
16. e.g., Bertrand Russell, *Principles of Social Reconstruction*, ch. IV.
17. *Open Society*, v. 1, pp. 169ff.
18. S.M. Lipset, *Political Man*, pp. 50, 417.
19. *Politics*, p. 9.
20. ibid., p. 41.
21. ibid., p. 53.
22. ibid., p. 16.

23. ibid., p. 17.
24. ibid., p. 44.
25. ibid., pp. 10ff.
26. ibid., p. 26.
27. ibid., p. 35.
28. Karl Marx, *Pre-Capitalist Economic Formations*, pp. 38ff.
29. *Politics*, pp. 251ff.
30. ibid., p. 215.
31. *Political Man*, p. 417ff.
32. Alexander Hamilton *et al.*, *The Federalist*, No. 10.
33. Notably in Niccolo Machiavelli, *The Prince*, passim.
34. Aristotle, *Nicomachean Ethics*, 1177b.

Chapter 2

1. J.G.A. Pocock, *The Machiavellian Moment* is still the standard account.
2. Pocock, op cit; Quentin Skinner, *The Foundations of Modern Political Thought*.
3. *Machiavellian Moment*, pp. 333ff.
4. *Prince and Discourses*, p. 62.
5. ibid., pp. 107–10.
6. ibid., pp. 349–51.
7. ibid., p. 108.
8. ibid.
9. ibid., pp. 147–58.
10. ibid., p. 122.
11. ibid., p. 119.
12. Sir James Harrington, *Oceana*, in *The Political Works of James Harrington*, pp. 165–6; *The Machiavellian Moment*, pp. 385ff qualifies what is all too briefly said here; Sir Francis Bacon, *The Essayes, or Counsells, Civill and Morall*, XXIX, 'Of the True Greatnesse of Kingdomes'. C.B. Macpherson, *The Political Theory of Possessive Individualism*, ch. IV offers yet another view.
13. *Essayes*, pp. 92–3.
14. H.T. Dickinson, *Liberty and Property*, pp. 91ff.
15. *Oceana*, pp. 161–5.
16. 'The Prerogative of Popular Government', *Works*, p. 405.
17. *Oceana*, pp. 159–60.
18. *Essays*, p. 48.
19. ibid., pp. 49–51.
20. ibid., pp. 499ff.
21. Bernard Mandeville, *The Fable of the Bees*, pp. 53ff.
22. ibid., pp. 329ff.
23. 'Of Refinement in the Arts, *Essays*, p. 284.

24. Robert Merton, 'Manifest and Latent Functions' in *Social Theory and Social Structure*, pp. 73ff.
25. ibid., pp. 126–29.

Chapter 3

1. Milton Friedman, *Capitalism and Freedom*, p. 10.
2. Thomas Hobbes, *Leviathan*, p. 95. J.N. Gray, *Hayek On Liberty*, ch II.
3. John Locke, *Two Treatises of Government*, pp. 378–9.
4. Robert Nozick, *Anarchy, State and Utopia*, p. ix.
5. *Politics and Vision*, pp. 286ff.; Hannah Arendt, 'What is Freedom?' in *Between Past and Future*, pp. 143–50.
6. Stephen Holmes, *Benjamin Constant and the Making of Modern Liberalism*, pp. 46ff.
7. Quentin Skinner, 'Negative Liberty' in R. Rorty, J.B. Schneewind and Q. Skinner, eds, *Philosophy in History*, pp. 212ff.
8. cf ibid. and Hannah Arendt, *The Human Condition*, pp. 207ff.
9. J.S. Mill, *On Liberty*, pp. 168–70.
10. *Anarchy, State and Utopia*, pp. 276ff.
11. *Hayek on Liberty*, pp. 125–8.
12. Hamilton *et al., The Federalist*, p. 45.
13. J.S. Mill, *Principles of Political Economy*, p. 754n.
14. ibid., pp. 766–7.
15. ibid., p. 767.
16. H.S. Maine, *Ancient Law*.
17. *Principles*, pp. 759–61.
18. *Liberty*, pp. 66–7.
19. See William Kornhauser, *The Politics of Mass Society* for a representative account of these fears.
20. John Rawls, *A Theory of Justice*, pp. 175ff.
21. *Anarchy, State and Utopia*, pp. 183ff.
22. ibid., pp. 198ff, 228–9.
23. e.g. *Hayek on Liberty*, pp. 69–75.
24. *Equality*, pp. 254ff.
25. 'The Probable Futurity of the Labouring Class', *Principles of Political Economy*, pp. 758–796; *A Theory of Justice*, pp. 258–74.

Chapter 4

1. Jeremy Bentham, *The Theory of Legislation*, pp. 199–210.
2. John Gray, *Mill On Liberty: A Defence*.
3. Jeremy Bentham, *Of Laws in General*, pp. 251ff.
4. A.M. Honore, 'Ownership', in A.G. Guest (ed.), *Oxford Essays in*

Jurisprudence, p. 113.

5. Robert Nozick, *Anarchy, State and Utopia*, p. 171.

6. James Grunebaum, *Private Ownership*, pp. 20–22.

7. James Mill, *An Essay on Government* in *Utilitarian Logic and Politics*, Jack Lively and John Rees, eds; cf. David Hume, *A Treatise of Human Nature*, Book III, pt iii.

8. *Essay on Government*, pp. 56–7.

9. Karl Marx, *Economic-Philosophical Manuscripts*, in *Early Writings*, pp. 375–9.

10. Anthony Crosland, *The Future of Socialism*, offers an (over-) optimistic perspective on this.

11. Richard Posner, *The Economic Analysis of Law*, pp. 29–30.

12. G.W.F. Hegel, *The Philosophy of Right*, pp. 47–8.

13. *Philosophy of Right*, p. 179.

14. *Theory of Legislation*, pp. 202–4; Orlando Patterson, *Slavery and Social Death*, *passim*.

15. J.S. Mill, *Representative Government*, pp. 198–9.

16. J.S. Mill, *Principles of Political Economy*, II, v, 2, p. 247.

17. John Locke, *Two Treatises of Government*, II, 22–4, 27, pp. 301–4.

18. *Principles of Political Economy*, II, ii, 7, p. 233.

19. cf. Alan Ryan, *Property and Political Theory*, ch. 8.

20. The classic account is A.A. Berle and G.C. Means, *The Modern Corporation and Private Property*.

Chapter 5

1. Robert Nozick, *Anarchy, State and Utopia*, ch 7.

2. Quoted in D.G. Ritchie, *Natural Rights*, p. 289.

3. ibid., p. 291.

4. *Two Treatises of Government*, II, 211ff, pp. 424ff; Locke allowed, of course, for a limited prerogative power, and thought *salus populi suprema lex*, which reduces any tension between general utility and individual right.

5. *Anarchy, State and Utopia*, pp. 174ff.

6. J-J. Rousseau, *Social Contract*, pp. 16–17.

7. *Anarchy, State and Utopia*, pp. 177ff.

8. *Two Treatises*, II, 7, p. 289.

9. Sir William Blackstone, *Commentaries on the Laws of England*, II, pp. 3–4.

10. Adam Smith, *The Wealth of Nations*, pp. 25–7.

11. cf J.S. Mill, *Liberty*, p. 150.

12. Ritchie, *Natural Rights*, pp. 263–71.

13. John Rawls, *A Theory of Justice*; R.M. Dworkin, 'Liberalism' in S.N. Hampshire (ed.), *Public and Private Morality*, pp. 128–31.

14. *Anarchy, State and Utopia*, pp. 177ff. Richard Tuck, *Natural Rights Theories*, pp. 58ff. (Where he shows how Grotius slowly came to this view from a much more 'Lockean' starting point.)
15. *Anarchy, State and Utopia*, p. 171.
16. ibid., pp. 150–53.
17. *Social Contract*, p. 199.
18. *Natural Rights*, p. 264.
19. *Two Treatises*, II, 23, p. 302.
20. *Natural Rights Theories*, pp. 77–8.
21. Cf Hart, 'Prolegomenon' with *Two Treatises*, above.
22. Joseph Raz, *The Morality of Freedom*, ch. I.
23. Dworkin, 'Liberalism', 130ff.
24. *Anarchy, State and Utopia*, pp. 58–9.
25. ibid., pp. 174ff.
26. ibid., p. 176.

Chapter 6

1. F.H. Bradley, 'My Station and Its Duties' in *Ethical Studies*, pp. 85ff.
2. E. Durkheim, *Professional Ethics and Civic Morals*, pp. 161ff.
3. Bernard Bosanquet, *The Philosophical Theory of the State* p. 142.
4. *Philosophy of Right*, p. 239.
5. ibid., pp. 131–2.
6. *Principles of Political Economy*, II, ii, 6, pp. 228–233.
7. Henry Sidgwick, *Elements of Politics*, pp. 55ff.
8. *A Theory of Justice*, especially, ch. VIII.
9. F.A. von Hayek, *Law, Legislation and Liberty*, vol. I.
10. Or to abolish it outright: Alasdair MacIntyre, *After Virtue*, pp. 240ff.
11. Roger Scruton, *The Meaning of Conservatism*, pp. 91ff.

Chapter 7

1. Herbert Spencer, *The Man versus the State*.
2. David Hume, 'Of Refinement in the Arts', p. 274.
3. *Of Laws in General*, pp. 251ff.
4. *Theory of Justice*, pp. 17–20.
5. *Elements of Politics*, pp. 142–50.
6. Hillel Steiner, 'Individual Liberty', pp. 35ff.
7. Alan Ryan, 'Liberty and Socialism' in B. Pimlott (ed.), *Fabian Essays in Socialist Thought*, pp. 105–110.
8. R.H. Tawney, *Equality*, pp 254ff.
9. David Hume, 'Of the Original Contract' in *Essays*, p. 457.
10. Bertrand Russell, *Freedom and Organization, 1815–1914*, pp. 347ff, 360ff.

11. Karl Marx, 'Of the So-Called Primitive Accumulation', *Capital*, I, Pt 8, pp. 873ff.
12. G.A. Cohen, *Karl Marx's Theory of History*, ch. IV.
13. *Anarchy, State and Utopia*, pp. 178ff.
14. G.A. Cohen, 'Capitalism, Freedom and the Proletariat' in Alan Ryan (ed.), *The Idea of Freedom*, pp. 8ff.
15. *Anarchy State and Utopia*, pp. 91–2.
16. *Wealth of Nations*, p. 687.
17. *Anarchy State and Utopia*, pp. 33–4.
18. ibid., pp. 158–9.
19. Isaiah Berlin, *Four Essays on Liberty*, p. 122n.
20. F.A. Hayek, *Law, Legislation and Liberty*, vol. II, pp. 85ff.
21. Alexander Herzen, *From the Other Shore*.
22. 'Liberty and Socialism', pp. 110ff.
23. *Karl Marx's Theory of History*, pp. 302ff.
24. L. Becker, *Property Rights*, pp. 75–80.
25. Ralph Miliband, *Marxism and Politics*, pp. 75–90.
26. Milton Friedman, *Capitalism and Freedom*, p. 10.

Chapter 8

1. cf F.H. Lawson, *The Law of Property*, pp. 35ff.
2. See Istvan Hont and Michael Ignatieff, eds *Wealth and Virtue* for some distinguished recent work on hese themes.
3. Ronald Meek, *Social Science and the Ignoble Savage*.
4. Adam Ferguson. *An Essay on the History of Civil Society*, p. 82.
5. H.L.A. Hart, *The Concept of Law*, ch V, 'Law as the Union of Primary and Secondary Rules'.
6. *Essay*, p. 84.
7. J-J. Rousseau, *A Discourse on the Origins of Inequality*, pp. 172–3.
8. *Essay*, p. 96.
9. ibid.
10. *Discourse on Inequality*, p. 199.
11. ibid.
12. J-J. Rousseau *The Social Contract*, p. 3.
13. 'Needs and Justice in the *Wealth of Nations*', *Wealth and Virtue*, pp. 2–7.
14. cf A.D. Hirschmann, *The Passions and the Interests*.
15. 'Needs and Justice', pp. 8ff.
16. Andrew Skinner, *A System of Social Science*, pp. 69–75.
17. David Hume, *A Treatise of Human Nature*, III, ii, 2.
18. *Treatise*, I, iii, 14; I, iv, 2.
19. *Discourse*, pp. 206ff.
20. *Discourse*, pp. 204–5.

21. *Treatise*, III, iii, 5.
22. above, p. 33; Hume, *Essays*, pp. 274-5.
23. J.G.A. Pocock, 'Cambridge Paradigms and Scotch Philosophers', *Wealth and Virtue*, pp. 235-7.
24. Bernard Mandeville, *The Fable of the Bees*, p. 64.
25. *Discourse on the Arts and Sciences*, pp. 130ff.
26. Immanuel Kant, *Idea for a Universal History from a Cosmopolitan Point of View*, p. 15.
27. G.W.F. Hegel, *The Philosophy of Right*, pp. 199-201.
28. Thomas Hodgskin, *Labour Defended Against the Claims of Capital*; Robert Owen, *A New View of Society*.
29. *Wealth and Virtue*, passim.

Chapter 9

1. Jeremy Bentham, *An Introduction to the Principles of Morals and Legislation*, ch I.
2. Richard Posner, *The Economic Analysis of Law*, pp. 17-19.
3. ibid., p. 9.
4. ibid., pp. 27-9.
5. ibid., p. 28.
6. Richard Coase, 'The Problem of Social Cost', *Journal of Law and Economics*, 1960, pp. 1-44.
7. *Economic Analysis of Law*, pp. 34-7.
8. ibid.
9. ibid., pp. 48-52.
10. H.S. Maine, *Ancient Law*.
11. A.W.B. Simpson, *An Introduction to the History of Land Law*, pp. 132-4, 225-9.
12. Robert Fogel and Stanley Engerman, *Time on the Cross: The Economics of American Negro Slavery*.
13. Eugene Genovese, *The Political Economy of Slavery*
14. Genovese, ibid., though as a good Marxist, he would not, of course, expect an economically dominant class to sell up.
15. P.D.G. Skegg, *Law, Ethics and Medicine*, pp. 232ff.
16. Roy Hattersley, *Choose Freedom*, pp. 99-101.
17. T.C. Schelling, *Choice and Consequence*, pp. 12-15.
18. Brian Barry, *Political Argument*, chs XIV, XV,
19. ibid., pp. 324-5.
20. *Anarchy, State and Utopia*, pp. 84-6.
21. *Political Argument*, pp. 234-5, 316-7.

Chapter 10

1. Jon Elster, *An Introduction to Karl Marx*, pp. 186ff.
2. G.W.F. Hegel, *The Philosophy of History*, p. 457.
3. G.W.F. Hegel, *The Philosophy of Right*, p. 279.
4. ibid., pp. 124–6.
5. Karl Marx, *A Contribution to the Critique of Hegel's Philosophy of Right* in *Early Writings*.
6. *Philosophy of Right*, pp. 197–201.
7. Karl Marx, *Economic-Philosophical Manuscripts*; *Contribution*, pp. 58ff.
8. *Contribution*, pp 60–62; *Manuscripts*, pp. 351–4.
9. Friedrich Engels, *The Origins of the Family, Private Property and the State*.
10. Karl Marx, *Capital*, I, 'Afterword'.
11. Karl Marx, *The German Ideology*, pp. 32–5.
12. Karl Marx, *Pre-Capitalist Economic Formations*, passim.
13. 'Manifesto of the Communist Party' in *Selected Works of Marx and Engels*, I, pp. 34–9.
14. ibid., p. 37.
15. *Economic-Philosophical Manuscripts*, pp. 359–60.
16. ibid., pp. 353, 377.
17. 'Excerpts from James Mill's *Elements of Political Economy*', pp. 277–8.
18. Harold Lydall, *Yugoslav Socialism: Theory and Practice*.
19. Cf *'Excerpts', pp. 276–8* and *On the Jewish Question*, pp. 230–31.

Bibliography

Arendt, Hannah, *Between Past and Future*, Faber and Faber, London, 1961.

Arendt, Hannah, *The Human Condition*, Chicago University Press, Chicago, 1958.

Aristotle, *Nicomachean Ethics*, in *The Works of Aristotle translated into English*, vol. ix, Clarendon Press, Oxford, 1915.

Aristotle, *Politics*, ed. E. Barker, Clarendon Press, Oxford, 1947.

Bacon, Sir Francis, *Essayes or Counsells, Civill and Morall*, ed. Michael Kiernan, Clarendon Press, Oxford, 1985.

Barry, Brian, *Political Argument*, Routledge & Kegan Paul, London, 1965.

Becker, Lawrence, *Property Rights*, Routledge & Kegan Paul, 1977.

Bentham, Jeremy, *An Introduction to the Principles of Morals and Legislation*, Athlone Press, London, 1970.

Bentham, Jeremy, *Of Laws in General*, Athlone Press, London, 1970.

Bentham, Jeremy, *Theory of Legislation*, ed. Bowring, Trubner, London, 1884.

Berle, A.A., and Means, G.C., *The Modern Corporation and Private Property*, 2nd edn, Harcourt, Brace, Jovanovich, New York, 1968.

Berlin, Isaiah, *Four Essays on Liberty*, Oxford University Press, Oxford, 1974.

Blackstone, Sir William, *Commentaries on the Laws of England*, Clarendon Press, Oxford, 1756.

Bosanquet, Bernard, *The Philosophical Theory of the State*, Macmillan, London, 1899.

Bradley, F.H., *Ethical Studies*, Clarendon Press, Oxford, 1876.

Coase, Richard, 'The Problem of Social Cost', *Journal of Law and Economics*, III (October, 1960).

Cohen, G.A., 'Capitalism, Freedom and the Proletariat' in Alan Ryan ed., *The Idea of Freedom*, Oxford University Press, Oxford, 1979.

Cohen, G.A., *Karl Marx's Theory of History*, Clarendon Press, Oxford, 1980.

Crosland, Anthony, *The Future of Socialism*, Jonathan Cape, London, 1956.

Dahl, Robert, *A Preface to Democratic Theory*, Chicago University Press, Chicago, 1956.

de Ste Croix, G.E.M., *The Class Struggle in the Ancient Greek World*, Duckworth, London, 1981.

Dickinson, H.T., *Liberty and Property*, Weidenfeld and Nicolson, London, 1977.

Durkheim, Emile, *Professional Ethics and Civic Morals*, Routledge & Kegan Paul, London, 1957.

Dworkin, Ronald, 'Liberalism' in Stuart Hampshire, ed., *Public and Private Morality*, Cambridge University Press, Cambridge, 1978.

Elster, Jon, *An Introduction to Karl Marx*, Cambridge University Press, Cambridge, 1986.

Engels, Friedrich, *The Origins of the Family, Private Property and the State* in *Selected Works of Marx and Engels*, Foreign Languages Publishing House, Moscow, 1963, II, pp. 187–327.

Ferguson, Adam, *An Essay on the History of Civil Society*, Edinburgh University Press, Edinburgh, 1966.

Fogel, Robert and Engerman, Stanley, *Time on the Cross: The Economics of American Negro Slavery*, Little Brown, Boston, 1974.

Fox-Genovese, Elizabeth and Genovese, Eugene, *Fruits of Merchant Capital*, Oxford University Press, New York, 1983.

Friedman, Milton, *Capitalism and Freedom*, Chicago University Press, Chicago, 1962.

Genovese, Eugene, *Red and Black*, Random House, New York, 1972.

Genovese, Eugene, *The Political Economy of Slavery*, Random House, New York, 1971.

Gray, John, *Hayek on Liberty*, Blackwell, Oxford, 1984.

Gray, John, *Mill on Liberty: A Defence*, Routledge & Kegan Paul, 1983.

Grunebaum, James O., *Private Ownership*, Routledge & Kegan Paul, 1986.

Hamilton, Alexander, Madison, James, Jay, John, *The Federalist*, Dent, London, 1937.

Harrington, James, *The Political Works of James Harrington*, ed. J.G.A. Pocock, Cambridge University Press, 1977.

Hart, H.L.A., 'Prolegomenon to the Principles of Punishment', *Proceedings of the Aristotelian Society*, vol. 60, 1959–60.

Hart, H.L.A., *The Concept of Law*, Clarendon Press, Oxford, 1962.

Hattersley, Roy, *Choose Freedom*, Michael Joseph, London, 1986.

Hayek, F.A., *Law, Legislation and Liberty*, 3 vols, Routledge & Kegan Paul, London, 1967.

Hayek, F.A. von, *Studies in Philosophy, Politics and Economics*, Routledge & Kegan Paul, London, 1967.

Hegel, G.W.F., *The Philosophy of History*, Dover Books, New York, 1956.

Hegel, G.W.F., *The Philosophy of Right*, Clarendon Press, Oxford, 1941.

Herzen, Alexander, *From the Other Shore*, Oxford University Press, Oxford 1979.

Hirschmann, Albert, *The Passions and the Interests*, Princeton University Press, Princeton, 1986.

Hirschmann, A.D., *The Passions and the Interests*, Princeton University Press, Princeton, 1977.

Hobbes, Thomas, *Leviathan*, Dent, London, 1914.

Hodgskin, Thomas, *Labour Defended Against the Claims of Capital*.

Holmes, Stephen, *Benjamin Constant and the Making of Modern Liberalism*, Yale University Press, 1984.

Hont, I. and Ignatieff, M., *Wealth and Virtue*, Cambridge University Press, Cambridge, 1983.

Hume, David, A Treatise of Human Nature, Clarendon Press, Oxford, 1888.

Hume, David, *Essays Moral Political and Literary*, Oxford University Press, London, 1963.

Kant, Immanuel, *On History*, Bobbs-Merrill, Indianopolis, 1963.

Klosko, Gabriel, *Plato's Political Thought*, Methuen, London, 1986.

Kornhauser, William, *The Politics of Mass Society*, Routledge & Kegan Paul, London, 1960.

Lawson, F.H., *The Law of Property*, Clarendon Press, Oxford, 1958.

Lipset, S.M., *Political Man*, Heinemann, London, 1960.

Lively, Jack and Rees, John, *Utilitarian Logic and Politics*, Clarendon Press, Oxford, 1978.

Locke, John, *Two Treatises of Government*, Cambridge University Press, Cambridge, 1967.

Lydall, Harold, *Yugoslav Socialism, Theory and Practice*, Clarendon Press, Oxford, 1984.

MacIntyre, Alasdair, *After Virtue*, Duckworth, London, 1981.

Maine, Henry, *Ancient Law*, John Murray, London, 1901.

Mandeville, Bernard, *The Fable of the Bees*, Penguin Books, Harmondsworth, 1970.

Marx, Karl, and Engels, Friedrich, *The German Ideology*, Lawrence and Wishart, London, 1963.

Marx, Karl, *Capital*, Penguin Books, Harmondsworth, 1974.

Marx, Karl, *Early Writings*, ed. L. Colletti, Penguin Books, Harmondsworth, 1973.

Marx, Karl, 'Manifesto of the Communist Party' in *Selected Works of Marx and Engels*, Foreign Languages Publishing House, Moscow, 1963, I, pp. 33–65.

Marx, Karl, *Pre-Capitalist Economic Formations*, ed. E. Hobsbawm, Lawrence and Wishart, London, 1964.

Meek, Ronald, *Social Science and the Ignoble Savage*, Cambridge University Press, Cambridge, 1976.

Merton, Robert, *Social Theory and Social Structure*, The Free Press, New York, 1968.

Miliband, Ralph, *Marxism and Politics*, Oxford University Press, Oxford, 1977.

Mill, J.S., *Principles of Political Economy*, in *Collected Works of John*

Stuart Mill, vols II, III, University of Toronto Press, Toronto, 1965.

Mill, J.S., *Utilitarianism, Liberty and Representative Government*, Dent, London, 1914.

Minogue, Kenneth, 'The Concept of Property and Its Contemporary Significance', in Pennock, J.R. and Chapman J.W., eds., *Nomos*, vol XXII, 'Property', New York University Press, New York, 1980.

Nozick, Robert, *Anarchy, State and Utopia*, Blackwell, Oxford, 1974.

Owen, Robert, *A New View of Society*, Penguin Books, Harmondsworth, 1969.

Patterson, Orlando, *Slavery and Social Death*, Harvard University Press, Cambridge, 1982.

Plato, *The Laws*, tr. R.G. Bury, Loeb, London, 1922.

Plato, *The Republic*, ed. F.M. Cornford, Clarendon Press, Oxford, 1941.

Pocock, J.G.A., 'Cambridge Paradigms and Scotch Philosophers' in Hont and Ignatieff, *Wealth and Virtue*, above.

Pocock, J.G.A., *The Machiavellian Moment*, Princeton University Press, Princeton, 1975.

Popper, K.R., *The Open Society and Its Enemies*, Routledge & Kegan Paul, London, 1945.

Posner, Richard, *The Economic Analysis of Law*, 2nd edn, Little Brown, Boston, 1977.

Rawls, John, *A Theory of Justice*, Harvard University Press, Cambridge, 1971.

Raz, Joseph, *The Morality of Freedom*, Clarendon Press, Oxford, 1986.

Reeve, Andrew, *Property*, Macmillan, London, 1986.

Ritchie, D.G., *Natural Rights*, Allen and Unwin, London, 1894.

Rorty, Richard, Schneewind, J.B., Skinner, Quentin, *Philosophy in History*, Cambridge University Press, Cambridge, 1984.

Rousseau, J-J., *The Social Contract and Discourses*, ed. G.D.H. Cole, Dent, London, 1913.

Russell, Bertrand, *Freedom and Organisation, 1815-1914*, Allen and Unwin, London, 1934.

Russell, Bertrand, *Principles of Social Reconstruction*, Allen and Unwin, London, 1916.

Ryan, Alan, 'Liberty and Socialism' in *Fabian Essays in Socialist Thought*, ed. B. Pimlott, Heinemann, London, 1984.

Ryan, Alan, *Property and Political Theory*, Blackwell, Oxford, 1984.

Schelling, Thomas C., *Choice and Consequence*, Harvard University Press, Cambridge, 1984.

Scruton, Roger, *The Meaning of Conservatism*, 2nd edn, Macmillan, London, 1984.

Simpson, A.W.B., *An Introduction to the History of Land Law*, Oxford University Press, Oxford, 1961.

Skegg, P.D.G., *Law Ethics and Medicine*, Clarendon Press, Oxford, 1984.

Skinner, Andrew, *A System of Social Science*, Clarendon Press, Oxford, 1979.

Skinner, Quentin, *The Foundations of Modern Political Thought*, Cambridge University Press, Cambridge, 1978.

Smith, Adam, *An Inquiry into the Nature and Causes of the Wealth of Nations*, Clarendon Press, Oxford, 1976.

Spencer, Herbert, *The Man versus the State*, Penguin Books, Harmondsworth, 1975.

Tawney, R.H., *Equality*, 4th edn., Allen and Unwin, London, 1952.

Tawney, R.H., *The Acquisitive Society*, Allen and Unwin, London, 1924.

Thucydides, *The Peloponnesian War*, Random House, New York, 1951.

Tuck, Richard, *Natural Rights Theories*, Cambridge University Press, Cambridge, 1979.

Walzer, Michael, *Spheres of Justice*, Martin Robertson, Oxford, 1983.

Wolin, Sheldon, *Politics and Vision*, Little Brown, Boston, 1961.

Zimmern, A., *The Greek Commonwealth*, Clarendon Press, Oxford, 1935.

Index